Evidence-Based Training Methods

Evidence-Based Training Methods

A Guide for Training Professionals

Ruth Colvin Clark, Ed.D.

Alexandria, Virginia

ASTD Press is an internationally renowned source of insightful and practical information on workplace learning and performance topics, including training basics, evaluation and return-on-investment, instructional systems development, e-learning, leadership, and career development. Visit us at www.astd.org.

Ordering information: Books published by ASTD Press can be purchased by visiting our website at store.astd.org or by calling 800.628.2783 or 703.683.8100.

Library of Congress Control Number: 2009940065

ISBN-10: 1-56286-704-0
ISBN-13: 978-1-56286-704-1

ASTD Press Editorial Staff:
Director: Dean Smith
Manager, ASTD Press: Jacqueline Edlund-Braun
Senior Associate Editor: Tora Estep
Senior Associate Editor: Justin Brusino
Editorial Assistant: Victoria DeVaux

Developmental Editor: Leslie Stephen
Indexer: Abella Publishing Services
Proofreader: Abella Publishing Services
Interior Design: Kathleen Schaner
Interior Production: PerfecType, Nashville, TN
Cover Illustration: Bruno Budrovic
Printed by Versa Press Inc., East Peoria, IL, www.versapress.com

Dedicated to Pete Sattig

Contents

Contents

Part V. What's Next?

Acknowledgements

This book would not have been possible without the support and resources from many individuals.

First, thanks to Jim Klein of the Department of Educational Psychology at Arizona State University. Without Jim's help getting access to literature databases I could not have obtained the many research studies that formed the basis for this book.

Second, if we did not have dedicated instructional scientists conducting and publishing research, there would be no evidence-based practice. I have cited many studies throughout the book. But in particular I want to recognize the substantial body of evidence from the laboratories of Richard E. Mayer of the University of California at Santa Barbara and John Sweller of New South Wales University. I have done my best to interpret their research and any errors in so doing are mine alone.

Third, I must recognize the talented sisters Ann and Stacy Kwinn who developed and produced the chapter cartoons. Also I am indebted to Dale Bambrick of Raytheon Professional Services for permission to use screen captures from their excellent e-learning courses.

Fourth, I thank the many individuals from ASTD who have helped shape and produce this book including Dean Smith, Jacqueline Edlund-Braun, Rhonda Crenshaw, and Ryann Ellis.

Last, my appreciation to Leslie Stephen, who is the best editor ever!

Introduction

Why Evidence-Based Practice?

A colleague called me recently and ended our conversation with a question: "Do you ever get frustrated? We know what to do! We know how to do it! Why can't our organizations let us do our job?" If your client has ever told you she needed a training program, it could not exceed 3 hours in length and it had to roll out in 3 weeks because work was slow at that time, then you know what I'm talking about. The root problem? Because everyone has been to school, everyone considers themselves an expert in training. For the most part we would not approach our physician telling them what treatment or medication we needed, not to bother with tests, and when it was convenient for us to take the medication. Why? Because the field of medicine is recognized as a profession!

A professional is one who makes decisions and takes actions based on a combination of personal experience, community wisdom, and valid evidence of what works. Only in the last 20 years do we have a useful body of research evidence to guide our training development and delivery decisions. And along with the evidence we have much clearer ideas of how learning occurs in the brain. Therefore we not only know what works, but we know why it works. However, to be of value, evidence must be accessed, interpreted, and disseminated. Training practitioners are busy. Most don't have time to find, read, and synthesize research. My goal in this book is to summarize the most up-to-date evidence we have on critical decisions you face every day.

If you are a classroom instructor, a developer of training materials, a training manager, or a designer or developer of any form of e-learning, this book is relevant to your work. I summarize research on the basic issues you face daily—such as proven methods to maximize learning with graphics, audio, and text; powerful universal instructional methods such as examples and practice; and evidence on best ways to organize your content.

Workforce learning programs expend over $100 billion a year in the United States alone! It's time to incorporate evidence and learning psychology into our program design, development, and delivery decisions. This book shows you how.

A Note About My Research Summaries

To make this book more readable, where practical, I've cited secondary compilations of research such as Mayer's 2009 edition of *Multimedia Learning* and my book, *Building Expertise*. These sources describe in detail and give citations for the research I summarize. At the end of each chapter, I list the specific relevant chapters in these secondary sources for readers who would like more detail.

How to Use This Book

First, get out your pencil and mark it up! I invite your active engagement. To that end I've inserted short questions throughout the chapters. These questions are designed to aid your processing of the information provided. Don't want to answer questions? No problem. You are in charge.

Second, review the chapters of greatest interest. I'd love it if you could read the entire book from chapters 1 to 14, but you simply may not have the time. From graphics to practice, each chapter deals with a specific stream of research on an important training issue or tactic. So feel free to use the table that follows this introduction to select the chapters of greatest relevance to your immediate needs.

Third, if you are really in a hurry, just skip to the back of each chapter. There I summarize in a checklist specific proven techniques you can apply to your training.

Finally, a request. Writing as a single author is a lonely endeavor. Let me know what was useful and your suggestions for improvement. You can reach me at Ruth@Clarktraining.com

Ruth Clark
Phoenix, Arizona
2010

Chapter Preview

Chapter Title	Chapter Topic
1. Training Fads and Fiction	Four common training myths, including learning styles and media panaceas. The type of evidence presented in the book including the limits of the research.
Part I. Learning and the Elements of Instruction	
2. Grounded Brain-Based Teaching	The features of working memory and long-term memory and how learning occurs in the brain.
3. Content Covered Is Not Content Learned	Three different learning goals and three instructional architectures to address each of those goals. Also discusses the three key components of all training to be addressed throughout the book: media, modes, and methods.
4. Architectures for Learning	In greater detail the three architectures introduced in chapter 3, including their features, benefits, and evidence for their use.

Chapter Title	Chapter Topic
Part II. Evidence-Based Use of Visuals and Words	
5. Visualize Your Content	The evidence behind graphics including the learning benefits of graphics, who benefits most from graphics, and what types of graphics are proven to improve learning.
6. Explain Visuals	The evidence supporting the best use of words (audio and text) to explain visuals.
7. Make It Personal	How you can leverage basic human social instincts in your training to maximize learning. Proven methods regarding the use of language, voice, and imagery to maximize social presence in learning.
8. Avoid Too Much of a Good Thing	How to eliminate extraneous visuals, words, and audio that defeat learning.
Part III. Evidence-Based Use of Examples and Practice	
9. Accelerate Expertise with Examples	How to leverage examples in your training in ways proven to improve both learning efficiency and effectiveness.
10. Maximize the Benefits of Practice	Five proven laws of practice in training related to the kinds, amount, and placement of practice exercises to maximize learning.

Chapter Title	Chapter Topic
Part IV. Leveraging Learning Architectures	
11. Giving Principled Presentations	How to avoid death by PowerPoint by applying proven guidelines discussed throughout the book to maximize the effectiveness of instructional presentations.
12. Building Stair-Step Lessons	How to maximize the effectiveness of highly guided lessons designed to build procedural skills.
13. Building Immersive Learning Environments	How to apply proven guidelines to create scenario-based lessons designed to build critical thinking skills.
Part V. What's Next?	
14. Beyond Training Fads and Fiction	The four training myths presented in chapter 1 in light of evidence discussed throughout the book with ideas on how to redirect resources currently wasted on those myths.

◆ ◆ ◆

Training Fads and Fiction

◆ ◆ ◆

Training Fads and Fiction

Do you talk on your cell phone while driving? If yes, you are among the 73 percent of drivers who do. But like seat belt use, your driving habits are about to change. Evidence shows that even hands-free cell phones are potentially lethal distractions putting you at four times greater risk of a crash!

Base training decisions on research evidence, not predictions.

by Ann Kwinn & C. Kwinn

In spite of the evidence, as of early 2009 only five states banned hand-held phones while driving. However, in 2009 the National Safety Council is calling on all states to outlaw use of mobile devices while driving. The journey from evidence to application of evidence is often slow and workforce learning is no exception.

We will see how evidence can save your organization time and money wasted on training fads that don't work, and at the same time can also guide you to invest your resources more productively in proven training methods.

Blood, Phlegm, Black and Yellow Bile

Our story starts in the early 1600s—the birth years of evidence-based practice. There are a number of examples from those years, but in line with the current popularity of vampires, I'll use blood. In the early seventeenth century, folks believed that blood was produced by the heart and the liver and was continuously used up by the body. In other words, there was no accurate conception of blood circulation. In 1628 William Harvey introduced the revolutionary idea that blood was not consumed by the body. Based on measures of blood volume and anatomical observations, he proposed that blood was pumped from the heart and circulated throughout the body returning again to the heart. Harvey, along with Galileo, Descartes, and others, turned the seventeenth century world upside down by advocating evidence and reason rather than traditional wisdom and faith as the basis for knowledge and decisions.

We've come a long way from the days when medical diagnosis and treatments were based on a balance of the four body humors of blood, phlegm, black and yellow bile. If you were lucky your treatment prescribed an amulet that at least did no harm. If you were not so lucky, you were subjected to bloodletting. Although great strides were made in medical science, over 400 years passed before health science professionals formally adopted evidence-based practice. Old habits die hard. Even though we've had evidence about the dangers of cell phones for more than five years, that data is just starting to be translated into policy changes regarding the use of mobile devices while driving.

What Do You Think?

Mark each statement below as Fad or Fact.

A. **Fad or Fact:** To accommodate different learning styles, it's best to explain a visual with words presented in text *and* in audio.

B. **Fad or Fact:** Instructor-led classroom training results in better learning than computer-delivered instruction.

C. **Fad or Fact:** Courses that get higher student ratings generally produce better learning outcomes.

D. **Fad or Fact:** Individuals with visual learning styles learn best from lessons with graphics.

E. **Fad or Fact:** Interesting stories and lesson themes promote learning.

What Is Evidence-Based Practice?

In the last part of the twentieth century, the medical profession was the first applied field to formally adopt the incorporation of evidence into clinical decisions. Sackett and colleagues (1996, 71-2) define evidence-based medicine as the "conscientious, explicit, and judicious use of current best evidence in making decisions about the care of individual patients." Only in the last 20 years has *evidence-based practice* migrated to the social sciences. In 1992 the American Psychological Association recommended that emerging clinical practice guidelines be based on both research data and clinical expertise. This initial statement evolved to the 2006 publication of "Evidence-Based Practice in Psychology" advocating a fundamental commitment to evidence-based psychological practice (APA Presidential Task Force 2006).

You might wonder whether evidence-based practice has any value for workforce learning. Unlike medical practitioners, most trainers do not see their work as having life or death consequences. Although there are some notable exceptions. Remember US Air 1549—the miracle of the Hudson? Here's what Captain Chesley "Sully" Sullenberger had to say: "One way of looking at this might be that, for 42 years, I've been making small regular deposits in this bank of experience: education and training. And on January 15, the balance was sufficient so that I could make a very large withdrawal" (CBS Evening News, February 10, 2009).

Even if you are not involved in safety-critical training, chances are your organization invests a great deal in workforce learning. In 2008 the United States alone allocated around $130 billion (Paradise 2009). What kind of return does your organization get on its training investment? Think of the last class that you developed or facilitated. To what extent did the content sequencing, training methods, and facilitation techniques promote learning? Many common training practices are based more on fads and fables than on evidence of what works. Let's look at the facts behind four of my favorite training myths.

Training Myth 1: Learning Styles

Like the four body humors of blood, phlegm, black and yellow bile, I think *learning styles* represent one of the more wasteful and misleading pervasive learning myths of the past 20 years. From audio learners to visual learners or from "sensors" to "intuitive," learning styles come in many flavors. Corporations and universities alike frequently incorporate the concept of learning styles and sometimes even use learning style assessments as part of their instructor training. For some reason, the idea of a learning style has a kind of cosmic intuitive appeal that is very compelling. Ask almost anyone whether they are a visual learner or a verbal learner and you will get an immediate commitment to a specific learning style!

The learning style myth leads to some very unproductive training approaches that are counter to modern evidence of what works. For example, many trainers believe that visuals should be described by words in text format for visual learners and narration mode for auditory learners. To accommodate visual and auditory learners a visual on a slide is explained with text and audio narration of that text. As we will see in chapter 6, this practice has been proven to actually depress learning.

The time and energy spent perpetuating the various learning style myths can be more wisely invested in supporting individual differences that are proven to make a difference—namely, prior knowledge of the learner. If you make one change as a result of reading this book, *give up the learning style myth!*

Evidence about Learning Styles

Do we have any evidence about learning styles? Kratzig and Arbuthnott (2006) compared the relationship among three learning style indicators.

They asked a group of university students to do three things. First, each participant rated their own learning style as visual, auditory, or kinesthetic. Second, each individual took a learning style test that classified them as a visual, auditory, or kinesthetic learner. Finally, each person was given three tests to measure visual memory, auditory memory, and kinesthetic memory. If the learning style concept had substance, we would expect to find some positive relationships among these measures. For example, someone who considered themselves a visual learner would score higher on the visual part of a learning styles test and have better memory for content presented visually. However, when all of the measures were compared, there were absolutely no relationships! A person who rated themselves an auditory learner was just as likely to score higher on the kinesthetic scale of the learning style test and show best memory for visual data. The research team concluded that "in contrast to learning style theory, it appears that people are able to learn effectively using all three sensory modalities" (Kratzig & Arbuthnott 2006, 241).

Another research study focused on sensing versus intuitive learning styles. Cook et al. (2009) compared learning of medical residents who tested as having a sensing learning style with learning of medical residents who tested as having an intuitive learning style. Each resident completed four web-based training modules on ambulatory internal medicine. Half the lessons started with a clinical problem followed by traditional information. The other half reversed the sequence, starting with information and ending with a clinical problem. Sensing learners should learn better with a case-first approach while intuitive learners should learn better from a traditional rule-example approach. Knowledge tests were administered at the end of each module as well as several months later. As in the experiment described previously, there was no association between learning style and instructional method. The research team concluded that "it appears from the preponderance of evidence that sensing-intuitive styles have little impact, if any, on educational outcomes" (88).

The lack of evidence about learning styles is the basis for my first recommendation.

◆ ◆ ◆

Fads & Fiction Guideline 1:

Do not waste your training resources on any form of learning style–based efforts including instructor training, measurement of learning styles, or training methods that attempt to accommodate learning styles.

◆ ◆ ◆

Training Myth 2: Media Panaceas

Only a few years ago, computer-delivered instruction incited a revolution in training. Of course computers were not the first technology to cause a stir. Decades prior to computers, radio, film, and television were hailed as having high potential for educational revolution. The first widespread dissemination of computer-based training (CBT) was primarily delivered on mainframe computers. Soon, however, advances in digital memory, display hardware, programming software, and Internet distribution catalyzed the rapid evolution of CBT to recent technological panaceas including web-based training, social media, digital games, and virtual worlds, to name a few. With each new technology wave, enthusiasts ride the crest with claims that finally we have the tools to really revolutionize training. And yet, if you have been around for a few of these waves, those claims begin to sound a bit hollow. In just a few years, today's latest media hype will fade, yielding to the inexorable evolution of technology and a fresh spate of technological hyperbole.

What's wrong with a *technology-centric view* of instruction? Instructional scientists have learned a lot about how humans acquire new knowledge and skills. Like Harvey, who gave birth to the modern mental model of blood circulation, instructional psychology has revealed the strengths and limits of a human brain which is the product of thousands of years of evolution. When we plan instruction around the latest technology gismo, we ignore the psychology of human learning which, as we have learned again with cell phones and driving, has severe limits. In fact, technology today can deliver far more information faster than the human brain can absorb it.

When we assume a technology-centric view, our focus is on all of the wrong things. Instead of designing training to support human learning processes, we get caught up in the latest technology trends without regard for how they can be most effectively used.

Evidence Against the Technology Panacea

For over 60 years, instructional scientists have attempted to prove the superiority of each new technology over old-fashioned classroom instruction. One of the first published media comparison studies appeared in the 1940s. The U.S. Army believed it could improve instructional quality and reliability by replacing many instructors with films. To its credit, before setting policy based on this idea, the Army tested it. It compared learning a simple procedure from a lesson delivered by film, by instructor, and by print. Each version used similar words and visuals. What do you think the studies found?

- ☐ A. Instructor-led training led to the best learning.
- ☐ B. Paper-based, the least expensive, led to the best learning.
- ☐ C. Films could replace instructors as they led to the best learning.
- ☐ D. Learning was the same with instructor, print, and film.

When the Army tested learners from each group, they discovered that participants from all three lesson versions learned the procedure equally well. In technical terms we say that there were "no significant differences in learning" among the three groups. Since that early experiment, hundreds of studies have compared learning from classroom instruction with the latest technology—the most recent being various forms of digital distance learning. In fact, so many media comparisons have been published, that a synthesis of all of the results (called a meta-analysis) found the same basic conclusion that the Army reported so many years ago: No major differences in learning from classroom lessons compared with electronic distance learning lessons (Bernard et al. 2004). Therefore, Option D is correct.

But wait! There is an important caveat to this conclusion. The basic instructional modes and methods must be the same in all versions. In other words, if the classroom version includes graphics and practice exercises, the computer version must include similar graphics and practice opportunities. That's because what causes learning are the psychologically active ingredients of your lessons regardless of what media you are using. Rather than asking which technology is best for learning, you will find more fertile ground by considering how instructional modes such as graphics and instructional methods such as practice can best promote learning. More than 50 years of media comparison research is the basis for my second recommendation.

Fads & Fiction Guideline 2:

Ignore panaceas in the guise of technology solutions in favor of applying proven practices on best use of instructional modes and methods to all media you use to deliver training.

As a postscript to this media discussion, what were once considered distinct and separate delivery technologies are increasingly converging. For example, Kindle merges books and computers. Handheld mobile devices merge functionalities of computers, newspapers, telephones, cameras, radios, clocks, and navigational devices to name a few. Will a time come when the media distinctions blur to the extent that this discussion becomes obsolete? Time will tell.

Training Myth 3: The More They Like It, the More They Learn

Do you collect student ratings at the end of your courses? Your answer is probably yes. Over 90 percent of all organizations use end-of-training surveys to gather participant evaluation of the quality of the course, the effectiveness of the instructor, how much was learned, and so on. These rating sheets are commonly called smile sheets, or *Level 1 evaluations*. If you are an instructor or a course designer, chances are you have reviewed ratings sheets from your classes. You might also have a sense of how much learning occurred in that class. Based on your own experience, what do you think is the relationship between participant ratings of a class and the actual learning that occurred?

- ☐ A. Classes that are higher rated also yield greater learning.
- ☐ B. Classes that are higher rated actually yield poorer learning.
- ☐ C. There is no relationship between class ratings and learning from that class.

To answer this question, researchers have collected student satisfaction ratings as well as lesson test scores that measure actual learning. They then looked to see what overall relationships surfaced. For example, did higher ratings correlate with more learning or less learning?

Evidence on Liking and Learning

A recent meta-analysis synthesized more than 1,400 student course ratings with student test data. Sitzmann et al. (2008) found there is in fact a positive relationship between ratings and learning. But the correlation was very small! In fact, it was too small to have any practical value. Specifically, the research team concludes that "Reactions have a predictive relationship with cognitive learning outcomes, but the relationship is not strong enough to suggest reactions should be used as an indicator of learning" (289).

What factors are associated with higher ratings? The two most important influencers of ratings are instructor style and human interaction. Instructors who are psychologically open and available—in other words who are personable—are associated with higher course ratings. In addition, the opportunity to socially interact during the learning event with the instructor as well as with other participants leads to higher ratings.

Evidence from comparisons of hundreds of student ratings and student learning outcomes is the basis for my third recommendation.

◆ ◆ ◆

Fads & Fiction Guideline 3:

Don't rely on course evaluations as indicators of learning. Use valid tests to assess the pedagogical effectiveness of any learning environment.

◆ ◆ ◆

Training Myth 4: Stories (Games or You-Name-It) Promote Learning

As I wrote this chapter, I happened to overhear a caller into a conservative talk radio show. "Those liberals," she claimed, "are just like teen agers—they act impulsively and don't think things out." I had to laugh at the blanket characterization of liberals, and it reminded me of many generalizations about various learning methods.

Have you heard that stories (or games or collaboration or you-name-it) are really good training techniques? Training lore is full of claims and recommendations about a variety of training methods like these. What's wrong with these kinds of recommendations?

First, we are using such broad terms for our techniques that statements about them are meaningless. Take games for instance. Do you mean puzzle games, adventure games, strategy games, or simulation games? Do you mean individual paper and pencil games, video games, or group participation games? As a category, games include so much diversity that it is just about impossible to make any generalizations about their instructional effectiveness. The same goes for many other instructional techniques such as graphics or stories.

Second, even if we narrow down to a fairly specific set of criteria for any given instructional method, its effectiveness will depend on the intended learning outcome and the learners. Is your goal to build awareness, to help learners memorize content, to teach procedural skills, to motivate, or to promote critical thinking? Regarding learner differences, prior knowledge (not learning styles!) is the most important factor that moderates the learning effects of instructional methods. Techniques that help novice learners are not necessarily going to apply to a learner with more expertise.

The lack of universal effectiveness of most instructional techniques is the basis for what I call the "No Yellow Brick Road Effect." By that I mean that there are few best practices that will work for all learners and for all learning goals. The evidence that has accumulated over years of research on general categories like graphics and games is the basis for my fourth recommendation.

◆ ◆ ◆

Fads & Fiction Guideline 4:

Be skeptical about claims for the universal effectiveness of any instructional technique. Always ask, How is the technique defined? For whom is it useful? For what kinds of learning outcomes does it work?

◆ ◆ ◆

What Is Useful Evidence?

As an undergraduate science major I have always been drawn to experimental evidence to guide our instructional decisions. Useful experimental evidence requires several conditions. First, subjects are randomly assigned to at least one experimental treatment as well as a comparison treatment. For example, from a pool of 50 students, 25 are randomly assigned to a multimedia lesson with background music while another 25 are randomly assigned to the same multimedia lesson with no background music. Random assignment assures us that individual differences among the learners are evenly distributed. For example, if our pool of 50 students included some who routinely liked and listened to music and some who preferred to study in silence, these differences would be "neutralized" in that there is an equal probability that both types would be assigned to the two lesson versions.

Second, our two lesson versions are identical in every respect except for the one variable of interest. Each lesson in our experiment would have exactly the same words and same graphics and would vary only in the presence or absence of music. By keeping everything consistent except for a single variable, we assure that differences in learning outcomes can be attributed to our experimental variable and not some other features of the lesson. If our experimental lessons had several differences other than background music, we would be comparing apples and oranges and could not really make any sense of the results.

After the learners complete the lesson, they are tested. The type of test is an important element of the experiment. Many educational experiments use a recall test in which learners are asked to write down what they learned. For workforce learning purposes, however, I prefer application types of tests that require the learners to use what they learned to solve a problem or complete a task. This is because in the world of workforce learning, we are most concerned with job-relevant application outcomes—not recall. Therefore in our music experiment, we would want to judge learning from a test that measured understanding and application of the lesson content—not just recall of content.

About Effect Sizes

I won't attempt a class on statistics here. But you need a couple of basic concepts to interpret the data I'll show you throughout the book. Let's start with *effect size*.

Suppose in our music experiment that on average the learners in the no-music group scored 80 percent while those in the music group scored 74 percent. On the surface, it seems as if learning is better without music. However, we need to do some statistical tests to determine whether a difference of six points is important enough to warrant a change in practice. Scientists report a statistic called effect size to help us make that determination. I'll be mentioning effect sizes throughout the book, so I'll give a brief explanation here.

Think of an effect size as a multiplier for the amount of variation (called a standard deviation) that occurs around an average set of scores. For example, suppose Sally scores an average of 60 percent with a standard deviation of 10 on lessons with background music. That means most of her scores fall between 50 and 70 percent (60 percent, plus or minus 10). If the effect size from our experiment on music is .8, then we can expect her score on average to increase from 60 to 68 percent (10 times .8 equals 8 points) when we eliminate background music.

Instructional scientists give us some guidelines regarding effect sizes summarized in table 1.1. As you can see, if the effect size is .8 or above, the results of the experiment are probably worth implementing. In contrast, for effect sizes below .3, there may not be sufficient value to warrant recommendations for practitioners. As you review the research I've summarized in this book or in other sources, always look at the effect size as one indicator of the practical implications of the results.

By the way, if you are now curious about the value of background music during learning, you can read about the actual experiments and results in chapter 8.

Table 1.1. Effect Sizes and Practical Significance

Effect Size	Practical Significance	The instructional method results in	Example: Average score of 70% with standard deviation of 10 points would change to
Below .3	LOW	less than 3/10 of a standard deviation improvement in learning	Average of less than 73%
.3 to .8	MODERATE	a 1/3 to 4/5 of a standard deviation improvement in learning	Average of 73% to 78%
.8 to 1.0	HIGH	a 4/5 to 1 standard deviation improvement in learning	Average of 78% to 83%
Above 1.0	VERY HIGH	a greater than 1 standard deviation improvement in learning	Average of more than 83%

Pooling Multiple Experiments with Meta-Analysis

If a recommendation to eliminate background music from multimedia lessons is based on one or two experiments our confidence in that recommendation must be somewhat limited. However, imagine that a large number of experiments were published that compared learning with and without background music. These experiments may have used different lesson content, included short and long lessons, and involved learners of different ages and backgrounds. If we find consistent results from lots of experiments we can feel much more confident that the results will apply to our learners and our lessons. A relatively recent technique called a *meta-analysis* pools the effect sizes of many individual experiments and derives generalizations based on many results.

Earlier in this chapter I reported the results of a meta-analysis of media-comparison experiments. Figure 1.1 plots the values of the effect sizes in 318 comparisons of learning from instructor-led lessons with lessons delivered by some form of electronic distance learning technology. As you can see in the histogram, most of the effect sizes fall in the near-zero range. In other words, most research studies found little learning difference among lessons taught in an instructor-led or computer learning environment. Data like this gives me a high degree of confidence in my guideline to avoid a technology-centric focus.

Limits of Evidence-Based Training

Although I'm a passionate advocate of using evidence as the basis for best practices in training, there are definitely some constraints we practitioners must consider. First, real world decisions cannot be made on the basis of evidence alone. Factors such as budget, development or delivery time constraints, technology capabilities, and political pressures are just a few of the realities most trainers must juggle. Second, the number of evidence-based principles available today is somewhat limited. After 20 years of concentrated research, Richard Mayer (2009) concludes: "Research in multimedia learning is still in its early stages" (279). Not only is the number of research studies limited, but the experiments themselves have

Figure 1.1. A Histogram of 318 Effect Sizes from Learning in Classroom Versus Electronic Distance Learning Media.

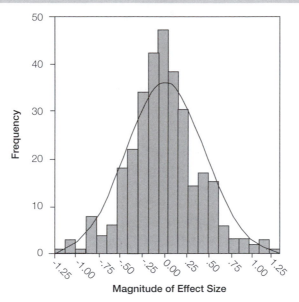

From Bernard et al. 2004.

limits. Most of them use Western (U.S., Australian, and European) college students as experimental students, and the outcomes may not apply to other cultures or age groups. In most cases, the experimental lessons are relatively brief, lasting from just a few minutes to an hour in length. We do not know the extent to which the conclusions derived from these relatively short lessons will apply to longer instructional events.

But we do have enough of a start for some firm recommendations that I make in the chapters to follow. As evidence accumulates, I anticipate that the guidelines I offer will be refined and perhaps in some cases even superseded. Nevertheless, the research efforts of the last 20 years lay the foundation for a science of instruction—a science that can offer practitioners a basis for minimizing resources wasted on the myths in favor of practices proven to enhance learning.

The Bottom Line

Let's conclude by revisiting the questions I asked in the beginning of the chapter:

What Do You Think?

1. **Fad or Fact:** To accommodate different learning styles, it's best to explain a visual with words presented in text *and* in audio.

    FAD. The benefits of using text and audio to describe visuals is a common misconception among trainers. In chapter 6, we will examine the evidence and psychology of how to best use words to describe visuals.

2. **Fad or Fact:** Instructor-led classroom training results in better learning than computer-delivered instruction.

    FAD. We saw the evidence from hundreds of media comparison studies that learning effectiveness does not depend on the delivery medium but rather reflects the best use of basic communication modes and instructional methods. We will be reviewing the evidence for these modes and methods in most of the chapters in this book.

3. **Fad or Fact:** Courses that get higher student ratings generally produce better learning outcomes.

    FACT—but only marginally. There is a very small positive relationship between ratings and learning. However, it is too small to draw any conclusions about the learning value of a class from student ratings of that class. Don't rely on student rating to assess the learning value of any training event.

4. **Fad or Fact:** Individuals with visual learning styles learn best from lessons with graphics.

    FAD. There is no evidence for the prevalent myth of learning styles such as visual learners and auditory learners. Perpetuating this myth detracts resources from more productive proven training methods to be described throughout the book.

5. **Fad or Fact:** Interesting stories and lesson themes promote learning.

FACT—sometimes. Yes, sometimes stories can be useful. However their value depends on the type of story, the outcome goal, and the placement of stories during learning. Remember, there is no Yellow Brick Road. We will look at evidence showing how some stories can actually depress learning in chapter 8.

Applying Evidence-Based Practice

The evidence I will review in this book can guide your decisions regarding the best instructional modes and methods to use in your training. But more important, I will consider the book a success if you become a more critical consumer of the various training recommendations appearing in practitioner articles, webinars, and conferences. My hope is that the next time you hear or read some generalizations about the latest technology or hot training method you will ask:

- ☐ What exactly are the features of this method?
- ☐ What is the evidence for this method?
- ☐ How valid is the evidence to support the method?
- ☐ For whom is the method most appropriate?
- ☐ How does the method fit with our understanding of the limits and strengths of human learning?

Let's take a look in chapter 2 at what we know about human memory and learning.

For More Information

Clark, R. (2008). *Building Expertise*, 3d ed. San Francisco, CA: Pfeiffer. See ch. 3.

Part I

Learning and the Elements of Instruction

In this section I start in chapter 2 by separating facts from fiction regarding how brains learn. In chapters 3 and 4, I introduce four basic components you will use to build learning environments:

- delivery media
- communication modes
- instructional methods
- design architectures.

◆ ◆ ◆

Grounded Brain-Based Teaching

◆ ◆ ◆

Grounded Brain-Based Teaching

Forty individuals drove a car in a simulator under four conditions: 1) no distractions, 2) talking on a handheld cell phone, 3) talking on a hands-free cell phone, and 4) intoxicated to 0.08 percent blood alcohol level. On a simulated freeway, a pace car braked 32 times during the 10-mile trip. Three of the participants who collided into the pace car were talking on cell phones both handheld and hands-free; none of the drunk drivers crashed (Strayer et al. 2006).

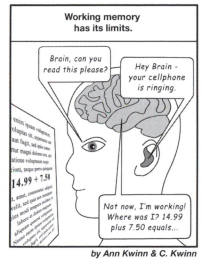

by Ann Kwinn & C. Kwinn

Research like this reveals the fragility of the human brain. Our brains are deceptive because we often don't realize the severe processing limits that affect all mental activities.

In this chapter we look at the psychology of learning and introduce the instructional accommodations trainers must make to leverage the strengths and weaknesses of the brain.

What Is Grounded Brain-Based Teaching?

Along with learning styles, another myth about individual differences is the popular concept of so-called left- and right-brained learners. While the idea of more logical (left-brained) versus more divergent (right-brained) approaches to tasks may have some useful applications, there is little science to support a literal right- and left-brain distinction. In this chapter, I introduce features and functions of human memory derived over the past 20 years from psychological experiments. In particular, we will look at proven mental learning processes that trainers must consider as they design, develop, and facilitate instructional events. It is these proven events and teaching methods that provide the basis for "grounded" brain-based teaching.

Limits of Human Memory

Let's try a short experiment. You need a pencil and paper. If you are near a friend or family member ask them to read List A in figure 2.1 to you. Ask them to read each word at a normal pace. When they are done, write down as many of the words as you can recall. If you are alone, spend about 30 seconds reading through the list of words yourself. Then without looking back, write down as many as you can recall. Next repeat the same process using List B in figure 2.2.

Figure 2.1. List A

1. House
2. Computer
3. Bird
4. Cloud
5. Scissors
6. Book
7. Dress
8. Marker
9. Bedroom
10. Chair
11. Calendar
12. Pink
13. Ocean
14. Gutter
15. Asia

Figure 2.2. List B

1. Ethics
2. Hire
3. Terse
4. Noun
5. Problem
6. Manage
7. Design
8. Retro
9. First
10. Solution
11. Color
12. Liquid
13. Pattern
14. Basic
15. Account

When done, count the number of words you recalled in each list. Which list was more memorable for you? Take a look at the two lists and consider what makes them different. Based on your review, select the correct answer below:

- ☐ List A has shorter words than List B.
- ☐ List A has more concrete words than List B.
- ☐ List A has more verbs than List B.

Most people recall more words from List A than from List B. In comparing the two, List B has a higher proportion of abstract words. The answer to the question above is the second option: List A has more concrete words.

Now look at the positions of the words you recalled in both lists. Determine whether the words you recalled came from the start of the lists, the end of the lists, or the middle. Do you see a pattern? If you reviewed the words sequentially from top to bottom, chances are you recalled more words from the start and end of each list.

The results from this little demonstration reveal three key features of our _working memory_—the memory that is both the engine and bottleneck of learning. The key features are summarized in table 2.1.

Table 2.1. Three Key Features of Working Memory

Feature	Description	What It Means
Active Processor	Working memory is the conscious part of your brain that thinks, solves problems, and learns.	Trainers must engage working memory for learning to occur.
Capacity Limits	Working memory can only hold a few items at one time. When working memory fills, it's processing capabilities slow down.	Trainers must avoid overloading working memory for learning to occur.
Dual Channel	Working memory has a separate area for storing visual and auditory information.	Trainers can extend working memory capacity by using the visual and auditory components.

Feature 1: Active Processor

First and foremost, working memory, as its name implies, is an active processor. It is the conscious part of your brain—the part that thinks, solves problems, and learns. It was the active processing of the words you read in the list that led to you recalling them later. The words you did not recall did not receive sufficient processing for learning.

Feature 2: Capacity Limits

Chances are you did not recall all of the words in either list. Working memory has pretty severe restrictions regarding how much information it can hold. And the limits are even more stringent when working memory is processing. Recent estimates set a limit of around three to five items when working memory must also be actively engaged in other activities. You recalled more words in the first part of the lists because your working memory had capacity to process those initial words. However, as you added more and more words, that processing capacity was soon exceeded. As each new word entered memory, it replaced an older word with little opportunity for processing. You may have recalled more of the last words in the list if you wrote them down right away. These last words were still active in working memory when you finished and were not replaced by more words.

Feature 3: Dual Channels

The term *dual channels* refers to the fact that working memory has a center for storing and processing auditory information and a separate center for visual information. When you read a concrete word such as *flower*, you are more likely to process it in two ways: as phonetic data and also as the image that your mind forms when reading the word. In contrast, a word such as *moral* is not as easy to visualize, and in many cases you encode it only in a phonetic format. Concrete words that can be encoded in two ways have a greater probability of being stored in memory. This is why List A with more concrete words was more memorable overall.

These three features—active processing, limited capacity, and dual channels—are the prime determinants for what works and what does not work in your training. We need working memory capacity to process new information for learning to occur. But when we load it up with content or irrelevant work, that processing is corrupted. We call this *cognitive overload* or *mental overload*. There are a number of techniques you can use to minimize cognitive overload that we will review throughout the book.

Long-Term Memory and Learning

While working memory is the star of the learning show, we can't leave out its supporting partner, *long-term memory*. Take a look at the chess board displayed in figure 2.3. Now imagine you look at it for about 5 seconds and then are asked to reconstruct it using a real chess board and all of the pieces. How many times would you need to refer back to the original chess board model? You won't be surprised that individuals like me, unfamiliar with chess, needed about seven to nine or more referrals to get most of the pieces correctly placed. However, what about a chess expert? Would they need to look back more or fewer times? Again, not surprising, chess masters

Figure 2.3. A Mid-Play Chess Board

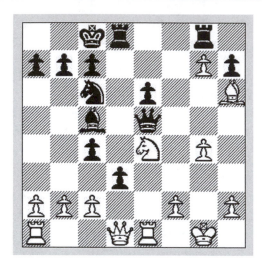

accurately replaced most of the pieces in about four tries. Why do you think that the chess masters had better memory for placement of chess pieces?

☐ A. Chess masters have better visual memory than chess novices.

☐ B. Chess masters have a higher intelligence than chess novices.

☐ C. Chess masters are more familiar with individual chess pieces than chess novices.

☐ D. Chess masters can draw on chess play patterns unavailable to chess novices.

To answer the above questions, the experimenters repeated the chess experiment with a crucial difference. Instead of using a realistic mid-play chess board, they substituted a scrambled board. The same number of pieces was placed on the board but *in a random order*. Again, they asked expert and novice chess players to recall the pieces. What do you think happened this time? Do you think the master players still had an advantage and needed fewer glances back at the model board? Or would the master and expert be equivalent in their memory?

The results were somewhat surprising. First, as you might expect, the novices needed about the same number of referrals as they did in experiment 1—seven to nine or more repetitions. But how about the experts? The experts actually needed *even more* opportunities to look back than did the novices!

These results support option D. For me and most novices, a chess board like the one shown in figure 2.3 holds about 24 chunks of information—each piece being a chunk. Since working memory can hold only around five or six chunks, naturally it takes me quite awhile to recall all of those pieces correctly. However, for an expert, there are many fewer chunks of information on the board. Why? Because the expert has played so much chess, they have a repository of play patterns stored in their long-term memory. Psychologists have estimated that chess experts store about 50,000 chess patterns in their long-term memory. Rather than recall each piece as a single entity as I did, they can recall whole clusters of pieces corresponding to various play patterns. However, when the pieces are placed randomly, those patterns not only don't help, they actually hinder recall performance. Chess experts look at a world that has become topsy-turvy and the conflict with their stored mental models actually makes their recall worse than novices.

From experiments like these we learn that unlike working memory, long-term memory has a huge capacity for information. During learning, whether formal or informal, the processing in working memory results in new or expanded patterns stored in long-term memory. These patterns can be brought back into working memory when needed and thereby endow working memory with a much larger virtual capacity.

Expertise and the Brain

Expertise in all domains relies on extensive patterns stored in long-term memory—patterns that enable experts to make much better use of the limited capacity of working memory. But sometimes those patterns get in the way. Have you ever watched a subject matter expert teach a class? Quite often they overload the learners' working memory with too much content, with unfamiliar terms, and with lengthy lectures. Experts just don't realize that their memories can hold and process information much more efficiently than novices. That's why an instructional specialist who knows less is a good partner for a subject matter expert—to help the expert break down their content into smaller pieces and add regular practice opportunities that allow learners a chance to process new content into long-term memory.

Automaticity: A Working Memory Bypass

We've seen that the patterns accumulated in long-term memory over years of experience afford experts the luxury of greater virtual working memory capacity. There is a second reason behind expert proficiency. It's called *automaticity*. Any task, physical or mental, that is repeated hundreds of times becomes hardwired into long-term memory. Any automated task can be performed with little or no working memory capacity. As you read this paragraph, you decode the words and sentences automatically and can allocate working memory to processing the meaning. Watch any first or second grader read and you will see a very different picture. Because word decoding is still not automated, reading is a very effortful process for these little ones. Only through years of practice are the many underlying skills of reading automated, allowing fast scanning of entire paragraphs in the mature reader.

Automaticity is the other secret of expert performance in any complex domain. Over years of practice, many layers of skills have automated allowing the expert to devote working memory to the coordination and problem solving needed to perform complex tasks. Automaticity allows multitasking. While familiar tasks such as decoding words are performed on automatic, the freed up capacity in working memory can be devoted to higher level tasks such as abstracting meaning.

However, as we have learned from the data on cell phones and injury accidents, automaticity is a dual-edged sword. For experienced drivers, routine driving is an automatic task freeing working memory to perform other tasks such as talking on a cell phone. When the basic driving tasks suddenly require the conscious attention of working memory, however, you may not be able to switch mental resources quickly enough to make a safe response. It is the psychological load imposed by talking on a cell phone as much as it is the physical activity of holding the phone that leads to cognitive overload. That's why a hands-free phone can be just as dangerous as a handheld set. I predict that once evidence catches up with policy, driving while using any kind of mobile device will be outlawed.

Grounded Brain-Based Teaching

Our instructional environments must support four key processes that transform information from instructors, workbooks, or computer screens into new knowledge and skills in long-term memory:

- attention
- processing in working memory
- management of mental load
- retrieval from long-term memory.

These core processes are the basis for grounded brain-based teaching. Let's take a little closer look at these four core events.

Focus Attention

All of us are familiar with lapses of *attention*. You might be reading this book and suddenly realize you did not process any of the meaning of the last two pages. You read the words but did not really process them. Or you are involved in a conversation, someone asks you a question and you realize you had not really been following the threads. Attention is the critical first step of any learning episode. Attention means that you have directed the limited capacity of working memory to a few specific elements in the environment. In the case of learning, you have directed your attention to the words and visuals you see and hear or to the actions you take during a practice exercise.

As instructors we use many techniques to gain and sustain attention. For example, we use a laser pointer or arrows on a slide to focus attention to the important elements of a complex visual. We also discuss the learning objectives of a lesson. By understanding the intended outcome goals, learners can direct attention to the more relevant portions of the lesson.

Not only do we help learners focus attention, but we also minimize the distractions that lead to split attention. Have you ever been reading a book and found the important visual needed to interpret the words on the back of the page? You flip over and study the visual, but at that point you can't see the words. How do you feel? Usually a little annoyed. That frustration is your working memory complaining about having to hold content in memory while accessing physically separated content needed to make the message meaningful. This is a common example of split attention that occurs not only in books but on slides and computer screens as well. Later, I will review evidence for techniques you can use to help learners focus their attention to what is relevant and also to minimize divided attention.

Engage Learners to Promote Processing

Just attending to a message, however, is not sufficient to ensure learning. Learning is an active process that takes place in working memory. By deeply processing the attended words and visuals in the lesson, the learner abstracts meaning from them and integrates them with existing knowledge in long-term memory. There are two main roads to help learners actively engage with the content. One is the use of frequent relevant activities that stimulate the active processing needed for learning. Practice exercises are the most common techniques. A second road is the use of what I call *implicit instructional methods*—methods that encourage deep processing in the absence of physical activity on the part of the learner. A good example is the use of relevant graphics. By sending a coordinated message with words and with visuals, you can leverage the dual channel feature of working memory and increase the opportunities for processing. In several chapters throughout this book I'll describe training methods proven to engage learners in ways that promote learning.

Manage Mental Load

Learning requires that the limited capacity of working memory be allocated to active processing. Therefore, effective learning environments minimize unproductive sources of mental load that bog down working memory. Unproductive mental load hogs working memory cap; does not contribute to learning. For example, we will see that .... comes to learning, less is often more. For instance, a simple line drawing will often lead to better learning than a realistic three-dimensional drawing, a photograph, or an animation. The reason is that working memory can abstract meaning from the simpler drawing without being overloaded by the extraneous information in more complex visuals.

Management of mental load is a fundamental prerequisite of all effective learning environments—especially when the content is complex and the learner is novice. Like the chess novices, learners who are new to the content lack the resources in long-term memory to form meaningful patterns and are more susceptible to overload than individuals with greater expertise.

Ensure Learning Transfer Via Retrieval

Transfer of learning means that after a successful training event in which new knowledge and skills have been stored in long-term memory, those new skills will be brought back into working memory when needed on the job. The access of knowledge and skills from long-term memory back into working memory at a later time is called *retrieval*. And retrieval is the psychological basis for transfer of learning. It's a mistake to assume that if learning takes place in the class transfer will occur. Just because your learners get an A on their test is no guarantee that they will be able to apply those new skills later. In fact, transfer of learning tends to be quite elusive and requires the use of special methods during training.

What if I ask you to state the months of the year? No problem, right? But now imagine stating the months of the year in alphabetic order. You could do it, but it would take you quite a bit of time to sort it out without writing the months down. The reason is that all retrieval cues are stored in long-term memory at the time of learning. In the case of the calendar, your cues are chronological—not alphabetic. As you plan your training environment, it's important to embed the right retrieval cues *at the time of* *learning*.

As I write this chapter I just reviewed a report that improper training contributed to the deaths of 50 people on Continental Flight 3407, the tragedy in Buffalo, New York. The pilot had received classroom training on how to handle an emergency such as the one he experienced but had never received simulation practice. It's possible that the classroom content was "learned" but stored as a type of knowledge that was not retrievable when urgently needed. The right retrieval cues were not there. Instead simulator training would have more effectively implanted performance-relevant retrieval cues and enough simulator training would have led to automaticity of response. For safety-critical tasks that do not occur on any routine basis in the workplace, periodic simulator and immersive learning environments are our best defense to build and refresh the skills needed to respond effectively.

The Bottom Line

Throughout this book, I'll discuss how you can use instructional modes and methods that promote learning. Rather than offer you traditional wisdom or fads, my recommendations will be based on evidence of what works as well as how those methods accommodate our brains. However, there are many questions you will have that won't be discussed in this book. To guide your decisions, ask yourself whether any approach you are considering is likely to support or corrupt one or more of the grounded brain-based learning and teaching processes I have summarized in this chapter.

Applying Grounded Brain-Based Teaching

As you plan your learning environment, ask yourself the following questions:

- ☐ What techniques can I use to focus attention to relevant content?
- ☐ Have I inadvertently split attention by physically separating related words and visuals?

☐ Have I fostered an active learning environment with a combination of relevant activities and implicit methods that promote processing?

☐ Have I avoided overloading my learners in ways that deplete working memory capacity needed for processing?

☐ Have I helped learners process new content in a way that will leave them with appropriate retrieval cues?

As you read through this book, you will revisit your initial reactions to these questions as we build a repository of instructional methods that accommodate the brain.

For More Information

Clark, R.C. (2008). *Building Expertise,* 3d ed. San Francisco: Pfeiffer. See ch. 4.

Mayer, R.E. (2009). *Multimedia Learning,* 2d ed. New York: Cambridge University Press. See ch. 3.

◆ ◆ ◆

Content Covered Is Not Content Learned

◆ ◆ ◆

Chapter 3

Content Covered
Is Not Content Learned

Some learning requires more than exposure.

This lady moves so awkwardly.

I think watching 'Dancing with the Stars' has really improved my dancing!

by Ann Kwinn & C. Kwinn

A stall occurs when the wing of an aircraft quits flying because the airflow that causes lift is disrupted. There are many reasons for a stall but the main remedy is to increase airspeed by lowering the nose of the aircraft. The pilot of Continental Flight 3407 responded exactly the wrong way to the stall warning by pulling the nose up and accelerating the stall. According to the head of the pilot training program of Colgan Air, the stall emergency response was "covered" in the ground school portion of training but never practiced in a simulator. Because "content covered" does not translate into content learned, 50 people died in Buffalo on February 12, 2009.

In this chapter we will look at three goals of training and introduce three training architectures to match each goal. We will also continue our delivery media discussion from chapter 1 by contrasting instructional media, modes, and methods.

Content Covered Versus Content Learned

Continental Flight 3407 was an especially tragic poster child for a widespread misconception—namely, that content covered translates into content learned. Often clients ask me to reduce the length of my four-day instructional design class to a two-day event. I usually respond: "Yes, I can cover the material in two days if I talk really fast and take out all of the practice. But your investment in the two days will be mostly wasted because content covered is not content learned."

Recall from chapter 1 that the U.S. annual investment in workforce learning approximates $130 billion. But that is actually a misleading number as it does not incorporate the most expensive element of training—the time that participants spend in the learning setting. For the most part, participants are on salary while in training and are not getting their normal work done—work that directly impacts the business bottom line. Therefore, clients often make training requests to achieve specific goals but limit the time they are willing to devote to the training. A common response among trainers is to create lessons that "cover" the content but eliminate the more time-consuming elements such as practice exercises. In most cases, the results of these decisions are not as catastrophic or public as an airplane crash. Nevertheless, the continued practice of covering the content erodes the integrity of any learning event that is designed to build workplace specific skills.

What do You Think?

Mark each statement you think is true:

☐ A. Active engagement is essential for learning.
☐ B. Content covered in a lecture will generally not result in learning.
☐ C. Some lectures are more effective than others.
☐ D. Delivery media affect learning outcomes.

What Is Content Covered?

When trainers say that they have covered the content, they usually mean the content has been presented usually in a lecture format often

accompanied by slides. Typically in these kinds of classes learner acti
is quite minimal. After her lecture, the instructor typically asks: "What
questions do you have?" Hearing none, she moves on to the next topic.
Managers, trainers, and students share an illusion of learning from an
event that offers little or no opportunity for overt engagement on the part
of the learner. What are the alternatives to a content-covered lesson and
when should those alternatives be considered? Let's look at three types of
knowledge and how different instructional environments can help learners acquire each.

Three Learning Goals

Table 3.1 summarizes three main learning goals: acquire knowledge, build
procedural skills, and build *strategic skills*. Knowledge refers to the concepts
and facts we have stored in long-term memory about a topic. Instructional psychologists call this type of content *declarative knowledge* because it
is easy to discuss or articulate. For example, in driver training you attend
class or read a booklet to learn facts and concepts such as speed limits,
road signs, right-of-way guidelines. The written portion of the driver's
test assesses your acquisition of this knowledge usually through multiple
choice questions.

Table 3.1. Three Learning Goals

Goal	Description	Example
Acquire Knowledge	Access and apply knowledge about work-relevant concepts, facts, and processes.	• Regulatory compliance guidelines • Names, parts, and functions of the Erylitizer • Features and benefits of new Product X
Build Procedural Skills	Can perform step-by-step routine tasks.	• Log into the system • Take a routine customer order • Perform routine maintenance
Build Strategic Skills	Can apply guidelines to diverse tasks that vary from instance to instance. Can engage in critical and creative thinking.	• Sell a new product • Troubleshoot an unusual failure • Create a website

ely on structures in long-term memory that support
—that is, tasks that are done more or less the same way
ing into your computer or following a recipe to make a
vo examples. As I mentioned in chapter 2, any procedure
at many times becomes hardwired into long-term memory.
At tha., . we say the skill is automated. Driving your car is a common
example of an automated skill. To acquire procedural knowledge, you
need to practice the task in a realistic workplace environment. You can't
learn to drive a car by reading the rules of the road or even by reading
the steps to drive. You actually have to drive the car—hopefully with an
instructor next to you. And you can't assess driving skill through a multiple choice test. That is why the driving test is a performance test with an
examiner sitting next to you.

Strategic skills also involve performance of tasks. However, unlike procedures, these tasks are not routine and require problem solving to adapt
to the unique circumstances of the situation. Making a sale and troubleshooting a unique equipment failure are two common examples. The
effective salesperson will adjust their approach based on their knowledge
of the client and the product features. Strategic skills are the most difficult
to train because the learning environment cannot exactly emulate the
performance environment. For example, in sales the client and product
mix will change each time. Training for strategic skills such as trouble
shooting typically involves four critical learning events:

1. reviewing important related knowledge, such as how equipment
    XYZ works under normal conditions

2. presenting a problem-solving process, such as document the prob-
    lem, verify the problem, isolate potential causes, and so on

3. studying examples that illustrate the problem-solving process
    applied to several examples, such as here is how an expert diag-
    nosed an ignition failure in the Model 310 mower

4. engaging in practice and feedback applying the process to several
    diverse scenarios.

Many job roles require a combination of declarative knowledge, procedural skills, and strategic skills. Each of these learning goals benefits from different instructional designs—designs I call *architectures*.

Three Instructional Architectures

To best help learners build the appropriate kind of knowledge and skill needed to perform their jobs, I recommend the use of three architectures: *show-and-tell, stair-step,* and *immersive.* These architectures vary regarding the design and methods of the training and are (for the most part) independent of the delivery media. For example, you can present a show-and-tell learning architecture in the classroom or in computer-delivered training. I introduce these architectures in this chapter and expand on their features, evidence, and psychology in chapter 4. At the end of the book in chapters 11–13, I give detailed guidance on how to build each.

Show-and-Tell Architectures

When instructors say they have covered the material, they are usually referring to a show-and-tell architecture that involves a lecture typically supported with PowerPoint slides. In a show-and-tell lesson, information is delivered to the learner who has minimal opportunity for overt engagement. A video documentary like the kind you see on the Science Channel or a traditional college lecture are two common examples of show-and-tell approaches.

As I mentioned previously, content covered is not necessarily content learned. Does that mean that show-and-tell architectures should never be used? No doubt you have experienced many show-and-tell events in your career and maybe even have delivered some. What is your opinion about show-and-tell architectures?

- ☐ A. They usually lead to minimal learning and should not be used.
- ☐ B. They can be effective for certain kinds of learning and should be used in moderation.
- ☐ C. They are the fastest way to deliver training and should be a dominant training approach.

In some situations show-and-tell learning environments are as effective as more interactive training. Haidet et al. (2004) compared how effectively medical residents learned to interpret diagnostic tests from two different lessons lasting about an hour each. One lesson was a show-and-tell lecture while the second more interactive version incorporated the same material but used group discussion of three case problems supplemented by instructor explanation. Learning was the same from the lecture as from the more interactive discussions. Keep in mind, however, that the event was relatively short (one hour) and that the learners were advanced not only in their field of medicine but in their learning skills. Similar to the chess experts I discussed in chapter 2, the medical residents were not overloaded by the content of the lecture and were able to assimilate their new knowledge into their long-term memory structures. Although those attending the show-and-tell event were not as physically active as were those attending the discussion-based event, they were psychologically actively processing the content.

My answer to the previous question is B. For learning facts, concepts, and processes such as how equipment works, a show-and-tell learning environment—when it uses optimal communication modes and instructional methods—can support psychological processing of the content. In chapters 5 and 6 I will show evidence to guide your presentations through the use of effective visuals and words to explain those visuals. Further, you can improve learning from a show-and-tell lesson by adding short response opportunities throughout. For example, in a large lecture setting, hand-held devices known as "clickers" can be used by students to respond to periodic questions from the instructor. Mayer, Stull et al. (2009) showed that clickers do improve learning from lectures. In my workshops, I place frequent short paper and pencil exercises in a workbook to give learners an opportunity to process the information delivered. Even in a traditionally passive medium such as this book, I have added periodic questions to encourage processing of the text.

The fallacy of show-and-tell learning environments is overreliance on them to support learning of procedural or strategic tasks—tasks that require active hands-on practice. The failure of show-and-tell architectures to lead to workplace skills is what I mean when I say: *Content covered is not content learned.* The misuse of show-and-tell training is the basis for my recommendation.

❖ ❖ ❖

Content Learned Guideline 1:

Use show-and-tell learning designs judiciously to teach facts, concepts, and processes related to job tasks. Add interactivity. Do not rely on show-and-tell environments to build job task proficiency.

❖ ❖ ❖

Notes

Stair-Step Architectures

Stair-step architectures, which I also call directive architectures or *part-task designs,* are learning environments that use a traditional sequence of explanation, example or demonstration, and practice with feedback. In short these lessons have a pattern of tell, show, do, and correct. Typically lessons are brief with each lesson focusing on specific steps to perform a task as well as any important facts or concepts related to those steps. For example, when teaching a lesson on how to log into a computer system, the concepts of log-in and valid password are followed by an instructor demonstration of the six steps to log-in and then hands-on computer practice using the same interface as the one used in the workplace. As the learners practice, the instructor reviews their steps and corrects errors.

Stair-step architectures are useful for building procedural skills especially for novice learners. The small steps and frequent corrective practice exercises minimize cognitive load. Of course, adding demonstrations and practice will take more time than merely covering the content. And any procedure that needs to be automated before performing it on the job, will definitely require more time devoted to drill and practice exercises. Often automation of skills can occur naturally in the workplace with normal repetition. Some skills, however, must be performed perfectly the first time. For example, a train engineer must respond immediately and without error to a track signal. Drill and practice on recognition and response to the signals will build automaticity prior to actually driving the train. For complex tasks that require rapid and errorless responses and when work practice opportunities are scarce because of either safety concerns or because relevant workplace situations are infrequent, procedural simulations can offer a useful drill and practice opportunity.

The evidence on the use of stair-step architectures is the basis for my next recommendation.

◆ ◆ ◆

Content Learned Guideline 2:
Use stair-step learning designs judiciously to help novice learners build procedural skills.

◆ ◆ ◆

Immersive Architectures

More contemporary course and lesson designs reflect an *immersive architecture* also called *guided discovery, problem-based,* or *whole-task design.* In an immersive learning environment, a realistic workplace problem or task assignment kicks off the lesson and serves as a context for learning. As students work to solve the problem, they are given instructional guidance such as a demonstration, expert advice, or even stair-step tutorials. The screen shot in figure 3.1 shows the interface for an online immersive case study for automotive technicians learning troubleshooting. The problem starts with a repair work order, and the learner has access to any of the objects in the virtual shop to conduct diagnostic tests. In chapter 13, I'll review this example in more detail with specific guidelines for constructing immersive lessons.

Immersive architectures are best suited for more advanced learners and for learning of strategic tasks that involve problem solving or creative design. These architectures can be applied to classroom or digital learning environments. When properly used, immersive architectures can motivate learners because of the immediate salience of the lesson relevance. However, when misapplied, learners may feel overwhelmed and lost.

Figure 3.1. A Virtual Shop Supports Troubleshooting Practice

Courtesy of Raytheon Professional Services LLC.

Unlike show-and-tell lessons that cover the content, immersive designs are learner-centered and have the potential to build a repertoire of job experience that in the real world could take years. In this sense, immersive designs can accelerate expertise.

We are still collecting evidence on when and how best to use immersive learning designs. At this stage, I offer the following recommendation.

◆ ◆ ◆

Content Learned Guideline 3:

Consider immersive designs to help experienced learners build a repertoire of strategic skills that would take a long time to acquire in the real world.

◆ ◆ ◆

Media, Modes, and Methods in Training

No matter which architecture or blend of architectures you are using, you will need to decide which mix of delivery *media* you will use, how you will communicate most effectively with the three *modes* of visuals, text, and audio, and which *instructional methods* will best help learners achieve the learning goals.

As I mentioned in chapter 1, delivery media are not the main determinants of instructional quality. Hundreds of media comparison experiments have shown that when the instructional modes and methods are the same, learning can be as good from a computer-delivered lesson as from a classroom lesson. The features and uses of media, modes, and methods in training are summarized in table 3.2.

What Are Modes?

By *modes*, I refer to the basic communication devices you will use to explain your content and present the instructional methods. Depending on your delivery medium, you have a choice of graphics, words presented in text, words presented in audio narration, and other audio such as music. For

Table 3.2. Three Training Components

Component	Description	Example
Delivery Media	Devices including instructors that deliver training.	• Computer • Video • Instructor • Book
Modes	Options to communicate content and instructional methods	• Visuals • Text • Audio
Training Methods	Techniques that support one or more of the psychological events of learning	• An arrow to direct attention • A practice exercise to encourage processing • An example to reduce cognitive load

example, if you are planning a podcast, you are limited to audio. If you are writing a book like this one, you are limited to text and a few graphics. In contrast, classroom instruction as well as many forms of computer-delivered training can include various forms of graphics (still and animated), text, as well as audio narration. In chapters 5–8 I'll summarize the evidence we have on how best to use these modes for learning purposes.

While media may not determine instructional quality, your media choices will constrain the modes you can use and can limit your use of proven instructional methods. For example, if you are comparing learning from an instructor-led event with a computer lesson and both use similar graphics, text, and audio, learning is likely to be equivalent. However if you compare learning from a computer lesson that uses graphics and audio to learning from a podcast that uses audio alone, the computer lesson will benefit from the learning advantages of visuals that I describe in chapter 5. That's why it's not quite true to say that delivery media have *no* effects on learning. The good instructor uses a mix of media to deliver the modes and methods that will support the learning outcomes.

What Are Instructional Methods?

An instructional method is any technique that supports the core learning processes of attention, active processing, cognitive load management, and retrieval. In other words, instructional methods aid learning. There are many, many instructional methods. Two very important methods are examples and practice exercises with feedback. Because of their importance and the wealth of evidence we have on these methods, I have devoted chapters 9 and 10 to them.

Just as all media cannot deliver all modes, similarly not all media can carry all methods. Take the critical instructional methods of practice and feedback. These methods can usually be delivered in a classroom setting (with access to appropriate equipment) and in many cases in computer-delivered instruction. However, media such as books and podcasts are much more limited in their capacity to promote practice and feedback. As you weigh your media options, consider the following recommendation.

◆ ◆ ◆

Content Learned Guideline 4:

Use a mix of media that can deliver the appropriate modes and instructional methods needed to help learners achieve the learning outcomes.

◆ ◆ ◆

The Bottom Line

Now that you have read this chapter, let's reconsider the decisions you made at the start. Take a minute to compare your initial answers with my responses:

☐ A. Active engagement is essential for learning.
TRUE. Active engagement is essential for learning, but the important engagement is psychological—not physical. In this book you will read about a variety of techniques you can use to promote productive psychological engagement.

☐ B. Content covered in a lecture will generally not result in learning.
FALSE. Actually content in the form of facts, concepts, and processes presented effectively in a lecture can result in learning of declarative knowledge. However, lectures are not appropriate as the sole resource for learning new skills.

☐ C. Some lectures are more effective than others.
TRUE. Some lectures are more effective than others. Lectures that embed some relevant interactivity as well as make best use of visuals and words will be more effective. In chapter 11, I give detailed guidelines for planning and developing effective presentations.

☐ D. Delivery media affect learning outcomes.
TRUE. Although media comparison studies have shown that the same learning can be realized from diverse media, the capability of different media to convey instructional modes as well as methods will constrain the effectiveness of a given medium.

Applying Content Learned to Your Training

Next time you get a request for training that includes a delivery time constraint, ask the client if you can take a little time to do a training needs assessment. Through that assessment, you can define the critical knowledge and skills that should be gained through the training, some background information on the intended learners, the delivery media alternatives, and at a high level the key instructional modes, methods, and architectures that are most appropriate.

If the delivery time your client has allowed for training is reasonable, put together your training plan and move ahead. If, however, the delivery time is unrealistically short and will require ill-advised shortcuts such as only covering the content, explain that content covered is not content learned and offer your client some alternatives. For example, a mix of self-study, working aids combined with on-the-job mentoring, and formal instructor-led learning can stretch the learning over several events. Or perhaps several short training sessions can be planned over a longer time period. Learners can be assigned some prework followed by a virtual classroom session. Next learners could meet in a face-to-face setting with follow-up work monitored by their supervisors or debriefed in a second virtual session. You can no doubt think of many alternatives to a suboptimal plan of "covering the content."

For More Information

Clark, R.C. (2008). *Building Expertise,* 3d ed. San Francisco: Pfeiffer. See ch. 2.

Clark, R.C., & R.E. Mayer (2008a). "Learning by viewing versus learning by doing: Evidence-based guidelines for principled learning environments." *Performance Improvement* 47, 5–13.

◆ ◆ ◆

Architectures for Learning

◆ ◆ ◆

Chapter 4

Architectures for Learning

Architecture: The structure of anything. Romanesque, Baroque, Art Deco. These are just three of over 30 different architectural styles.

A combination of art and science, great architectures are both functional and aesthetic. Instructional architectures are no different. Usually documented as an outline or lesson plan, learning blueprints reflect assumptions about learning that differ as to 1) sequencing of content; 2) size of topics; 3) role of the learner; and 4) role of the instructor.

Effective structures—including learning environments—start with a blueprint.

We saved time by skipping the blueprint phase.

by Ann Kwinn & C. Kwinn

In this chapter I will expand upon the three architectures of learning introduced in chapter 3: *show-and-tell* (or expository), the *stair-step* (or part-task), and *immersive* (or whole-task) architectures. We will review details about the features, evidence, and psychology for each architecture to help you select the best combination for your training goals.

Blueprints for Training

From the ancient Pantheon to Frank Lloyd Wright's Fallingwater house, all memorable structures start with a blueprint. The dimensions, the style, the materials—all the major elements that define the final structure are encoded in the blueprint. Likewise, learning environments consciously or unconsciously embed an instructional architecture. Usually documented as outlines or lesson plans, learning blueprints vary on some fundamental assumptions about learning that translate into differences in the roles of the learner and instructor and on content sequence and segmenting. In this chapter we will contrast the design features, evidence, and applications for the three most common learning architectures.

What Do You Think?

Review the outlines for three Excel lessons in figure 4.1 and then mark the statements that you think are correct.

- ☐ Lesson Outline A is the LEAST effective lesson plan.
- ☐ Lesson Outline B is the MOST effective plan for all learners.
- ☐ Lesson Outline C is a more effective plan for experienced learners.
- ☐ All three lesson plans are effective because they all include the same content.

What Is a Lesson Architecture?

In chapter 3 I introduced instructional architectures defined as design plans that differ regarding the role of the learner, the role of the instructor, the philosophy of learning, as well as how content is chunked and sequenced. Here we will get into more detail about these architectures. In table 4.1, I summarize the main features that differ among the three architectures.

Instructor-Centered Versus Learner-Centered Plans

Architectures vary regarding the type and amount of *overt learner activity* from very low levels to very high levels. When overt learner activities are

Figure 4.1. Three Excel Lesson Outlines

Lesson Outline A	Lesson Outline B	Lesson Outline C

I. What is a spreadsheet?
  A. Columns & rows
  B. Cells
  C. Cell references
II. What is a formula?
  A. Formats
  B. Operators
III. How to set up a calculation
  A. Addition-subtraction
  B. Division-multiplication
  C. Order of operations
  D. Demonstration
	I. What is a spreadsheet?
	  A. Columns & rows
	  B. Cells
	  C. Cell references
	  D. Practice 1: Cell references
	II. What is a formula?
	  A. Formats
	  B. Operators
	  C. Practice 2: Writing formulas
	III. How to set up a calculation
	  A. Addition-subtraction
	  B. Division-multiplication
	  C. Order of operations
	  D. Demonstration
	  E. Practice 3: Calculations
		I. Calculate monthly sales
		  A. Demo: Pat—Jan
		  B. Rows, columns, cells, cell references, adding
		  C. Assignment: Pat—Feb
		II. Calculate monthly commissions
		  A. Demo: Pat—Jan
		  B. Formulas, multiply
		  C. Assignment: Pat—Feb
		III. Calculate annual net income
		  A. Demo—Pat
		  B. Order of operations
		  C. Assignment: Janet

relatively low, the instructor activity is high. We call this an instructor-centered approach. Look at lesson outline A in figure 4.1. It is an example of a show-and-tell architecture. In this plan the instructor explains and illustrates the core concepts and demonstrates their use. In other words the instructor does just about all of the work. Learning will occur only if the attendees process the words and visuals themselves. Show-and-tell architectures are also called expository designs and predominate the lecture teaching method. The traditional view of show-and-tell architectures is an instructor dispensing knowledge onto sponges that soak it up.

In contrast, Excel lesson outline B divides activity between instructor and learner with the instructor orchestrating the event. Learning plans that start with explanations from the instructor followed by practice assignments for the learners follow a stair-step pattern. In stair-step architectures the instructor is the director explaining, illustrating, assigning, and correcting student work.

Table 4.1. A Comparison of the Features of Three Core Instructional Architectures

Architecture	Learner Activity	Traditional Role of Instructor	Modern Role of Instructor	Segmenting and Sequencing	Attitude toward Errors
Show and Tell	Little or no overt activity; Learning relies on mental activity	Dispenser of knowledge	Dispenser of knowledge and methods to encourage mental processing	Varied	NA since no practice
Stair Step	Practice with corrective feedback assigned after each content chunk	Provide stimuli in the form of questions to elicit correct responses which are rewarded	Manage mental load and promote mental processing with short topics and frequent practice plus corrective feedback	Bottom up sequencing of basic topics building to more advanced; topics segmented into small chunks	Errors are minimized by providing immediate corrective feedback when mistakes are made
Immersive	High learner activity as lesson is driven by a task assignment	Architecture is new so no traditional role	Promote learning in work-realistic context; provide guidance as needed	Holistic approach in which knowledge and skills are integrated into solving of job tasks	Errors are considered an opportunity for learning

Features

Lesson outline C requires the most overt learner activity because each lesson begins with a spreadsheet task assignment. Lessons that begin with a problem to solve or a task to complete are examples of an immersive design plan. In an immersive architecture the learner's role is that of active problem solver while the instructor coaches and provides guidance as needed. In lesson outline C the instructor offers guidance primarily through a demonstration of an Excel task. An immersive architecture uses a much more inductive approach assuming that experience is the best path to learning.

Content Organization and Sequence

In show-and-tell and stair-step architectures the content is broken into small topics and sequenced in a logical prerequisite order. For example topic A is presented before topic B, as shown in figure 4.2. In contrast, the immersive architecture uses a whole-task organization in which task demonstrations and assignments provide a context for learning knowledge topics and steps. In this approach associated knowledge topics are learned in the context of a whole-task demonstration or assignment as shown in figure 4.3.

Figure 4.2. Stair-Step Architectures Build Skills Via Topics

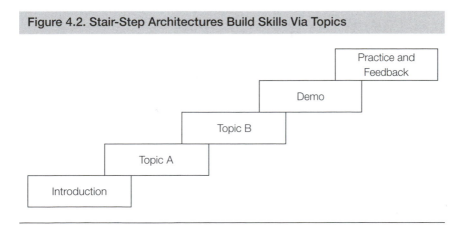

Figure 4.3. Immersive Architectures Use Realistic Work Tasks to Drive Learning

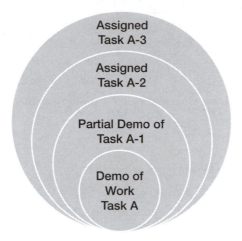

Show-and-Tell Architectures

In chapter 3, I emphasized the limits of show-and-tell architectures with the theme: *Content covered is not content learned.* Show-and-tell architectures, however, represent the most common training technique in use today. Whether it be an instructor lecture in a classroom or through a webinar or a self-study online presentation, why do you think show-and-tell architectures are so popular?

Here's what I think. First, we teach the way we were taught. Since lecture is the most prevalent method used in school, we naturally emulate what we know. The second reason is time. It's much faster to put together a presentation than to prepare lessons that include practice and feedback. As I mentioned in chapter 3, training professionals are often assigned ambitious goals to be achieved in very limited time frames. To accommodate stakeholders they cover the material with a show-and-tell plan bypassing more time-intensive methods such as practice exercises. Given that these factors are unlikely to change in the near future, we should invest effort to use show-and-tell events wisely and build them to be as effective as possible.

What Are Lectures Good For?

In figure 4.4, I summarize data presented by Bligh (2000) from several experiments that compared different types of learning from lectures versus other architectures or methods. The far left set of bars shows how lecture compared to a stair-step architecture when the learning goal was acquistion of information. The second to the left set of bars shows how lecture compared to class discussion when the goal was promoting thinking skills. The third to the left set of bars shows how lecture compared to practice to learn a skill and the right-most graph shows student preference for lectures compared to stair-step architectures.

Figure 4.4. How Lecture Compared with Other Methods for Different Learning Goals

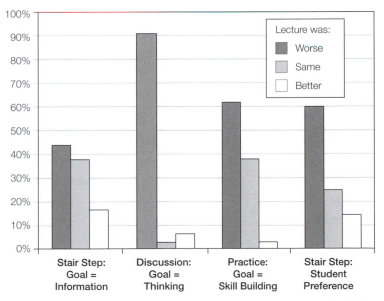

Based on data from Bligh, 2000.

In summarizing his review of the research Bligh (2000) concludes that "the balance of evidence favors the conclusion: Use lectures to teach information. Do not rely on them to promote thought, change attitudes, or develop behavioral skills" (20). Expository instruction in the form of lectures or online presentations can be as useful as other methods to teach facts, concepts, and even processes. In other words, lecture can effectively teach information. You can see on the left-most bars of the chart that lecture was the same as or better than a stair-step method in 55 percent of the experiments when the goal was information acquisition. Onboarding, product knowledge updates, compliance training, and dissemination of new policies and work rules are just a few examples of information-dominant training that can be effectively taught using a show-and-tell method.

Unfortunately, show-and-tell learning is too often misapplied when the desired outcome goal is to promote thinking or build behavioral skills. Compared to discussion, lecture was a poorer method to promote thinking in 90 percent of the experiments. Compared to practice, lecture was a poorer method to teach behavioral skills in 60 percent of the experiments. For promoting thinking or building behavioral skills, turn to stair-step or immersive learning plans.

Stair-Step Architectures

The stair-step design, also called a part-task approach, is the most common learning architecture after the show-and-tell method. Most software training applies a stair-step design. As the name applies, the lessons reflect a building block structure with a sequence of key concepts taught prior to the main lesson task. The Excel lesson outline B in figure 4.1 illustrates a stair-step design. Notice that the lesson starts with a fundamental concept—What is a spreadsheet—along with several subtopics including the main structural components of a spreadsheet: rows, columns, and cells. Next, the key concept of a formula is taught along with associated subtopics. Following these basic concepts, the main lesson task—to set up a calculation in the spreadsheet—draws on the supporting topics and integrates them into the final task. Each topic builds on the previous topics. For example, when discussing formulas, the concept of cell references is included.

The stair-step architecture has a very directive style. Learners are handheld with some detailed explanations, some examples or demonstrations, and then a highly guided practice exercise. Notice in the sample Excel lesson outline B, practice exercises are included with each topic. During the practice, the instructor monitors learners correcting errors as they go. The assumption is that learners need to practice the new skills and the fewer errors made during that practice the better. Immediate corrective feedback on exercises is a critical feature of this approach.

In contrast, an immersive architecture takes a much more hands-off approach encouraging learners to attempt tasks and learn from mistakes.

Immersive Architectures

In an immersive architecture, also known as a whole-task design, the instructor releases a lot of control and allows learners much more freedom. Excel lesson outline C illustrates an immersive architecture. Notice that rather than start with small topics such as columns and rows, the lesson begins with a simple spreadsheet demonstration followed by a similar task assignment. For example, the first assigned task involves a simple addition calculation. While learning how to perform the addition task, the concepts of row, column, and cell are introduced. The goal of an immersive architecture is to teach all of the same content as the stair-step approach but in the context of authentic work tasks. By learning the topics in the context of the whole task, training relevance is more salient and transfer to the job may be more direct.

However, learning the content while simultaneously performing even a simple job task runs the risk of imposing too much mental load. The learner is required to orchestrate several things at once. Therefore, the immersive architectural plan may be best suited to learners with some relevant background knowledge and must incorporate ample support and guidance.

Comparing Architectures

In summary, there are two main differences that distinguish show-and-tell, stair-step, and immersive architectures. The first difference concerns the roles learners must assume: 1) processing delivered content mentally in a show-and-tell architecture, 2) responding to frequent exercises and corrective feedback in the heavily guided stair-step architecture, and 3) autonomous problem solving in immersive architectures. These learner roles have complementary instructor roles as well. In show-and-tell, the instructor dispenses knowledge, but to maximize potential for learner processing of that knowledge the instructor should use instructional methods that promote mental processing. In the stair-step architecture, the instructor dispenses knowledge, assigns practice, and corrects learner errors. In the immersive design, the instructor offers support as needed while learners complete task assignments.

The second main difference concerns sequencing of topics. Supporting topics are sequenced first in stair-step architectures, whereas they are incorporated into task demonstrations and assignments in the immersive architecture. Additionally, content topics tend to be quite small in stair step and may vary in size in the immersive approach.

Architectures and the Brain

How do these three different architectures affect the brain? Remember the four core learning processes discussed in chapter 2—attention, processing in memory, management of mental load, and support for learning transfer. How do the architectures score on their support for each of these processes? In table 4.2, select the level of support you think is offered by each architecture. After you review the discussion, return to the table and change any of your ratings.

Attention
All things being equal, I rate the show-and-tell architecture as offering the least support for attention. It will come as no surprise that student

Table 4.2. Circle the Level of Learning Process Support Each Architecture Provides

Process	Architecture								
	Show and Tell			Stair Step			Immersive		
Attention	High	Medium	Low	High	Medium	Low	High	Medium	Low
Processing in Working Memory	High	Medium	Low	High	Medium	Low	High	Medium	Low
Load Management	High	Medium	Low	High	Medium	Low	High	Medium	Low
Learning Transfer	High	Medium	Low	High	Medium	Low	High	Medium	Low

attention as measured by heart rate declines rapidly over time in a lecture setting. Because of passivity, focus wanders. In contrast, the stair-step architecture, organized by brief topics punctuated by frequent responses, will sustain attention more effectively. As the most learner-centered of the architectures, the immersive design demands continuous engagement and is likely to promote high levels of learner attention. In table 4.2 I rate show-and-tell as low and stair-step and immersive designs as medium to high. As a result, it's especially important to use instructional methods that stimulate and focus attention in show-and-tell lessons. I'll discuss some useful techniques in chapter 11.

Processing in Working Memory

Learning—especially knowledge learning—can occur in show-and-tell architectures. But learning in show-and-tell relies primarily on what I call *implicit instructional methods* that stimulate mental processing rather than the overt learner activity promoted in the other two architectures. For example, an appropriate visual added to a presentation is an implicit method that can dramatically increase learning. Because they require overt learner responses, both the stair-step and the immersive plans stimulate processing in memory. In table 4.2 I rate show-and-tell low to medium and the stair-step and immersive plans as high.

Managing Mental Load

The stair-step design offers the most support to manage mental load for several reasons. First, the topics are short. Second, topics build on one another with the easiest topics followed by more complex. And, third, explanations are followed by activities to encourage processing of those topics. Because of the high degree of load management, stair-step designs are most effective for novice learners.

The immersive design runs a greater risk of overloading learners since it asks learners to work on a task and learn at the same time. For this reason, the immersive design is often more appropriate for learners with some background knowledge who are not as at risk for overload.

Because it does not provide opportunities for overt processing of content, the show-and-tell architecture can also easily overload working memory capacity to absorb new information. For this reason, it's a good idea to keep expository segments brief and to use techniques to reduce mental load.

In table 4.1, I rate the stair-step method as offering a high level of load management support and show-and-tell as well as immersive as offering low to medium levels.

Promoting Transfer of Learning

Remember from chapter 2 that transfer of learning depends on the encoding of the right cues at the time of learning. In the calendar activity in chapter 2, it was not that easy to list the months of the year in alphabetic order because your learning cues were chronological. The immersive design attempts to teach new knowledge and skills almost totally in context. By assigning the learner a job-realistic task, the learning is contextualized throughout the event.

Context is also the key to the transfer potential of stair-step and show-and-tell architectures. Because topics are presented as separate entities in these architectures, invest extra effort to integrate the topics in a job-realistic context such as with a case-study assignment or kickoff discussion.

In table 4.2, I rate the immersive and stair-step architectures as high in support of transfer and show-and-tell as low to medium depending on how much workplace context is included.

We see that each of the architectures has potential risks and tradeoffs. As a general rule, show-and-tell architectures are best suited to teach facts and concepts, whereas the other two architectures lend themselves to teaching new skills. The stair-step design is better suited for novice learners and for learning of routine tasks, and the immersive design best fits groups with more experience whose work benefits from critical thinking skills associated with strategic tasks. The effects of the architectures on the brain are the basis for my first recommendation.

◆ ◆ ◆

Architecture Guideline 1:

Use a show-and-tell architecture to teach concepts and facts. Use a stair-step design for introductory lessons that focus on routine skills. Use an immersive design for more advanced lessons that involve critical thinking skills.

◆ ◆ ◆

Evidence for Architectures

Imagine that you are a new medical student. As you enter medical school you can select a traditional curriculum consisting of basic science lecture classes accompanied by laboratory work. Alternatively, you can opt for a problem-centered curriculum in which you learn in the context of solving patient case studies. As you work through the different cases, the anatomy, physiology, and pathology are taught in the context of the scenarios. Which curriculum would you prefer? Which curriculum would lead to better learning?

Medical schools were one of the first educational domains to embrace a type of whole-task architecture known as *problem-based learning*. Initiated at McMaster University in Canada in the 1970s, problem-based medical education is now ubiquitous not only in medical schools but in other educational domains such as economics, law, and other health science professions.

Because medical students are extensively evaluated, we've learned the most about immersive architectures from medical education. In a nut shell, problem-based learning and a traditional science class approach lead to similar learning of science knowledge and facts among medical students. However, the immersive approach leads to earlier development of clinical problem-solving skills, and medical students like it better than the traditional science curriculum approach. What might account for the popularity of problem-based learning? I think the main reason is relevance. A medical student has already studied years of science and is now focused on a career objective. By engaging with patient cases early on, the instructional environment is more in tune with their career goals. Keep in mind that medical students have already completed many years of education and have a defined professional focus. Therefore, the increased popularity of problem-based learning among medical students may not apply to your learners.

An Experimental Comparison of Stair-Step and Immersive Architectures

Although problem-based learning has shown some advantages in medical education, those results may not apply to other domains. Lim and his colleagues (2009) compared learning Excel skills from a stair-step architecture with learning the same skills from an immersive design. The learners were student teachers, and the course goal was to use Excel to construct a grade book. One group of learners was assigned to a stair-step plan like the Excel lesson outline B in figure 4.1 and an alternative group was assigned to an immersive design. In the immersive class, learners built an Excel grade book—first watching an instructor demonstration, next creating it themselves using the same data, and finally creating another grade book using different data. The class was instructor-led and involved two one-hour sessions. After completing the two sessions, all students took three tests: a skill component test that measured ability to perform 16 small Excel tasks, a whole-task test that required learners to construct a grade book, and a transfer test that required learners to use Excel to construct a budget. Take a look at the results in figure 4.5 and select which interpretations below reflect the data.

☐ A. The whole-task architecture was the most effective approach.
☐ B. The part-task architecture was the most effective approach.
☐ C. The whole-task architecture led to better transfer of learning.
☐ D. The whole-task architecture better prepared learners to construct a grade book.

As you can see from the bar graph, the part- and whole-task lessons were equally effective for learning of the individual Excel skill components. However, the whole-task approach led to somewhat better achievement on the grade book construction test and *much better* achievement on the budget test. If you answered C and D, you read the results correctly.

Figure 4.5. Learning Excel Skills from Part- and Whole-Task Architectures

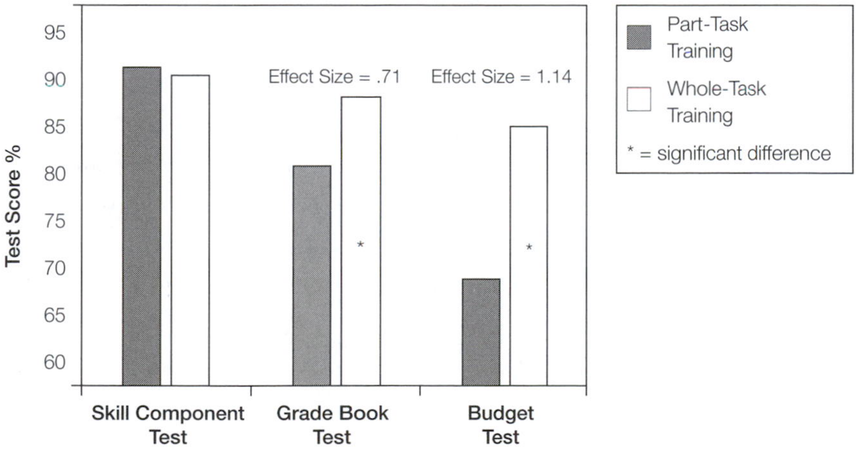

Lim, Reiser, Olina, 2009.

Better scores on the grade book test among whole-task learners likely resulted from the four opportunities they had to construct a grade book compared to the single opportunity the part-task learners had at the end of their second session. The better scores on the budget test show that the whole-task approach holds promise for transfer of learning to more diverse situations than the part-task approach. Perhaps learning component skills in the context of Excel tasks helped learners build a more integrated understanding of how Excel works with any form of data.

Accelerating Expertise with Immersive Architectures

Kumta and his associates (2003) found that final-year medical students scored better on their exams when online immersive cases were added to their normal curriculum of lectures, bedside tutorials, and outpatient clinics. A series of eight web-based clinical problems solved during a three-week orthopedic rotation required students to comment on radiographs, interpret clinical and diagnostic test results, and provide logical reasoning to justify their clinical decisions. It's not surprising that the group getting immersive online cases learned more than those who did not. After all, expertise comes primarily from experience, and the students working with online cases got more experience.

Workforce learning in domains where real-world practice is either unsafe or unavailable may especially benefit from the expertise boost that immersive architectures can provide. Managed health care is decreasing the amount of time patients spend in hospitals leading to reduced opportunities for clinical practice. Learning to troubleshoot unusual equipment failures can be a challenge since by definition these failures are rare. By creating multiple cases with diverse simulated faults, troubleshooting expertise can be accelerated. Finally, teaching new military officers good planning and execution techniques on the battlefield through case studies offers opportunities to consider situations that are infrequent and for which the cost of error is high. Figure 4.6 is one screen from an immersive multimedia lesson designed for new Army officers to teach effective planning and critical thinking skills relevant to combat situations.

Figure 4.6. An Immersive Multimedia Course for New Combat Officers

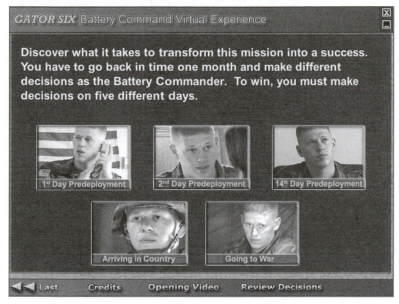

With permission from Wills Interactive.

Because immersive learning architectures are relatively recent, we do not have a wealth of research on their effectiveness. However, based on results to date, I offer the following recommendation.

◆ ◆ ◆

Architecture Guideline 2:

Consider immersive architectures to accelerate expertise especially when access to realistic job experience is limited or impractical.

◆ ◆ ◆

The Bottom Line

We started our discussion with a comparison of three Excel outlines shown in figure 4.1. Now that we have discussed the three architectures, reconsider which option below is true:

☐ Lesson outline A is the LEAST effective lesson plan.

TRUE. Lesson outline A reflects a show-and-tell approach to teaching Excel and is the least effective architecture for this learning goal. It does not include any opportunity for practice, and therefore skill building would likely be minimal.

☐ Lesson outline B is the MOST effective plan for new learners.

TRUE. Lesson Outline B uses a stair-step approach. You see a series of topics that gradually build. Learners have frequent opportunities to practice each lesson topic. This outline is most likely the best approach for individuals who are new to spreadsheets because it manages mental load most effectively.

☐ Lesson outline C is a more effective plan for experienced learners.

TRUE. Lesson outline C teaches the same topics but embeds them in a series of Excel tasks that learners must tackle. Therefore, lesson outline C reflects an immersive or whole-task approach. I would recommend this approach for learners with some relevant experience with spreadsheets.

☐ All three lesson outlines are effective since they all include the same content.

FALSE. Although all three lesson outlines include the same content, the sequencing and segmenting of the different architectures will have different effects on different learners.

Applying Architectures

There are no bad architectures. Each has its strengths, drawbacks, and applications. Chances are many of your training programs use two or sometimes even all three of these approaches. Ask yourself the following questions as you consider your design mix:

1. Is my goal to build a skill?
   —Is the goal performance of a routine skill and are the learners relatively novice? If yes, consider a stair-step design.
   —Is the goal performance of a strategic skill based on critical thinking? If yes, and especially if the learners have some experience, consider an immersive design.

2. Is my goal to teach facts, concepts, and processes?
   —If yes, consider a show-and-tell approach. Use instructional
   methods that will support the brain as you plan the presentation.

No matter which architecture or combination of architectures fit your situation, you will need to communicate with the modes of visuals, text, and audio. In the next chapters we will examine evidence on how best to use these modes. Likewise, all of the architectures can benefit from the instructional method of examples. We will look at how best to design examples in chapter 9. If you are using a stair-step or immersive design, practice activities will be a major component. Chapter 10 is devoted to evidence on effective practice exercises.

In chapters 11–13, I will integrate many of the evidence-based guidelines offered in chapters to follow with detailed guidelines and examples of how to prepare a lesson based on each of the three architectures.

For More Information

Bligh, D.A. (2000). *What's the Use of Lectures?* San Francisco: Jossey-Bass.

Clark, R.C. (2008). *Building Expertise*, 3d ed. San Francisco: Pfeiffer. See ch. 2.

Lim, J., R.A. Reiser, & Z. Olina (2009). "The effects of part-task and whole-task instructional approaches on acquisition and transfer of a complex cognitive skill." *Educational Technology Research & Development* 57, 61–77.

Part II

Evidence-Based Use
of Visuals and Words

In this section I summarize the evidence and psychology about how best to use three fundamental communication modes of visuals, audio, and text in your learning environments.

◆ ◆ ◆

Visualize Your Content

◆ ◆ ◆

Chapter 5

Visualize Your Content

No matter which learning archi- tecture you use, slide after slide of text and more text makes for a boring event. And slides and screens that are walls of words fail to leverage one of the most powerful tools proven to boost learning: Graphics!

As training professionals, most of us have concentrated on verbal rather than visual literacy. Our lack of visual skills as well as time and resource constraints has left our learning landscapes devoid of graphics.

by Ann Kwinn & C. Kwinn

In this chapter I review the learning value of adding graphics to words. We will consider what kinds of learners most benefit from visuals as well as the kinds of visuals that leverage the brain for learning.

The Lost Potential of Graphics

Why do we see so many slides or screens filled with text? Chances are you will hear one of the following reasons:

- Text is much faster to create.
- I'm not an artist.
- My content does not lend itself to visuals.

If you are like most trainers, you are very comfortable in a world of words. Since preschool your education has focused on verbal literacy. We all devoted many hours to reading and writing from the primary grades all though college. In contrast, most of us have had no training in visual literacy! We think and communicate with words rather than graphics.

I have a colleague who produces nature videos that feature animals in exotic settings. When I asked her how they got those beautiful visuals that fit the documentary theme and narration so perfectly, she chuckled, "Oh, no. We shoot lots and lots of visuals and then we write the story to match them." In video, the visuals drive the story. In the world of workforce learning, the job must drive the story. But the more you can visualize the job content, the better for learning. I've found some of the best e-learning developers have a background in video production. Why does a video background help new e-learning developers? Because video relies so heavily on the eyes, one has to think visually from the start. Same goes for e-learning. Computer screens cry out for visual treatments.

But you don't need to be a video production expert to leverage the power of graphics. You just need to take the time to apply some basic guidelines as you build your learning environments.

What Do You Think?

Put a check next to each statement about visuals that you believe is true:

- ☐ A. When you add visuals to text, learning improves.
- ☐ B. Decorative or thematic visuals increase interest and learning.

☐ C. Some learners benefit from visuals more than other learners.

☐ D. Not all visuals are equally effective.

What Is a Graphic?

For our purposes, I define a *graphic* as a two- or three-dimensional visual representation of lesson content. This includes typical lesson visuals intended to directly represent the content such as a screen capture from a software application or a line drawing of equipment. It also includes more abstract visuals to summarize lesson ideas such as a tree diagram to show organizational relationships or a 3-D computer-generated schematic animation of a how an engine works. Graphics may be simple such as a line drawing or complex such as a photograph. Graphics may be presented in a still format or may incorporate motion as in an animation.

As you can see, graphics of various types can offer considerable visual diversity to a lesson. In most cases adding visuals to text in your lessons will increase production time and costs of your materials. You might wonder whether there is a payoff to that investment. Let's take a look at the evidence for including visuals in learning environments.

Can Graphics Boost Learning?

We have quite a bit of research evidence to buttress investments in visuals. Mayer (2009) has conducted many experiments that compared learning from a lesson in which the content was delivered exclusively with text to learning from the same lesson that added a visual to the text. For example, figure 5.1 shows one segment from a lesson on how a bicycle pump works with and without a visual.

After reviewing either the text only or the text plus graphics lesson version, college students completed a problem-solving test. In all cases the lesson with visuals led to better learning for a median effect size of 1.4! That means if a typical lesson with no visuals resulted in an average test

Figure 5.1. Text (A) and Text and Graphics (B) Versions from Lesson on Pumps.

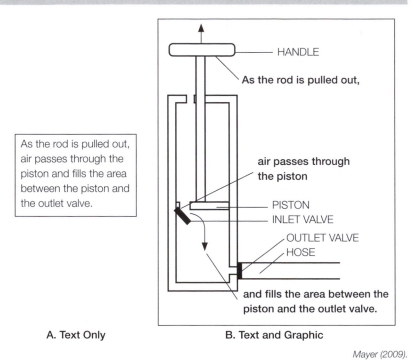

As the rod is pulled out, air passes through the piston and fills the area between the piston and the outlet valve.

HANDLE

As the rod is pulled out,

air passes through the piston

PISTON
INLET VALVE
OUTLET VALVE
HOSE

and fills the area between the piston and the outlet valve.

A. Text Only   B. Text and Graphic

Mayer (2009).

score of 75 percent with a standard deviation of 10, the same lesson with relevant visuals added would yield an average score of 89 percent—a gain of 14 points! Gains like these mean your investment in useful visuals has a high potential to translate to a substantive payoff in learning.

Graphics and the Brain

I mentioned in chapter 1 that in 1628 William Harvey was the first to document an accurate description of blood circulation. Understanding of processes like blood circulation reflects an accurate knowledge representation stored in long-term memory. Knowledge stored in long-term memory that depicts a complex process such as blood circulation is called a *mental model*. Researchers have asked students to draw pictures and describe how blood circulates through the heart. From the drawings and descriptions, the researchers identified mental models ranging from flawed to incomplete to accurate. The most primitive mental models called ebb and flow reflect the idea of blood moving from the heart to the body and back again but lack any specific mechanism for doing so. A more sophisticated model—the single loop—incorporates the idea of blood flowing from the body into the heart and then from the heart back into the body but leaves out the lungs. The correct mental model—double loop—includes the process of unoxygenated blood entering the heart from the body, being pumped to the lungs, returning to the heart with oxygen and then being pumped back to the body.

Butcher (2006) compared the effects of different lesson versions on circulation mental models like these. Similar to the bicycle pump experiment described previously, she compared learning from lessons that described blood flow with text alone to learning from lessons that added diagrams of circulation through the heart. She contrasted the learners' drawings and descriptions of blood circulation before and after the lessons. As with the bicycle pump experiments, the lessons that included a graphic resulted in greater improvement of circulation mental models compared to lessons with text only. In other words, visuals help learners build a more accurate understanding of blood circulation.

To analyze the "thoughts" learners had while studying, she recorded comments they made while reviewing the lessons and tallied all inferential comments that connect and extend ideas stated in the lesson. For example, one student read the following text: "As the blood flows through the capillaries in the body, carrying its supply of oxygen, it also collects carbon dioxide. The blood that empties into the right atrium is dark colored. It has picked up carbon dioxide from the body cells." From this text, the student made this inference: "The blood is dark because of the carbon dioxide . . . oxygen probably enriches the red color of the blood." In

Figure 5.2. Inferences on Blood Circulation Produced in Three Lesson Versions

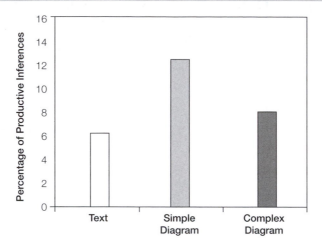

Based on data from Butcher, 2006.

figure 5.2, I show a graph of the percentage of statements that included productive inferences.

Take a look at her data and select the option(s) below that accurately summarize(s) the results:

- ☐ A. Adding diagrams helped learners generate more inferences.
- ☐ B. Both simple and complex diagrams led to more inferences than no diagram.
- ☐ C. Simple diagrams helped learners make more inferences than complex diagrams.

Learners studying the lessons with diagrams made a higher percentage of productive inferences compared to learners reviewing text alone. Statements A, B, and C are all true. In chapter 8 we will consider why the simple diagram was more effective. For now, we can conclude that diagrams stimulate the brain to generate correct inferences during study, which in turn lead to increased comprehension.

The amount of evidence showing the learning benefits of adding visuals to text supports my first recommendation.

◆ ◆ ◆

Graphics Guideline 1:

Promote deeper learning by adding visuals to text.

◆ ◆ ◆

When diagrams are added to text, learners are able to develop a more complete, more accurate mental model by making correct inferences about the relationships presented in the lesson. Useful visuals work because they offer the brain an additional opportunity to build mental models.

Who Benefits from Graphics?

Do all learners benefit equally from graphics? Based on your own experience as a learner and an instructor, select the options below that you believe are true:

- ☐ A. All learners benefit from adding visuals to words.
- ☐ B. Visual learners benefit more from adding visuals to words.
- ☐ C. Novice learners benefit more from adding visuals to words.

As I discussed in chapter 1, a pervasive training myth is the idea that some learners are visual while others are auditory. Learners who see themselves as visual learners believe they learn more from visuals, and learners who see themselves as auditory believe they learn more from words presented in narration. In reality, all learners *who are new* to a content area benefit from a relevant visual. However, experienced learners don't gain much from adding visuals to words. Why? Imagine that you have worked with bicycle pumps and are familiar with them. As you read a text description of how the pump works, your brain can easily visualize the words. In other words, you are able to generate your own visual representation as a result of your prior knowledge. In contrast, the novice does not know enough about a bicycle pump to form accurate images. Statement C above is the only true statement.

Several experiments show that visuals that benefit novices don't help experts. For example, Brewer and his colleagues (2004) compared understanding of judicial instructions presented with words alone (audio instructions) with instructions presented with words and visuals (audio-visual instructions). If you have ever served on a jury, you know that the judge gives a verbal explanation regarding the legal aspects of the case to consider during deliberations. Brewer's experiment included two types of mock juries: one made up of typical citizens and another made up of law students. The lesson consisted of about 10 minutes of a judge's auditory instructions for a self-defense trial. The audio-visual version added a flow chart and visuals that corresponded to the judge's explanations. For example, to illustrate the requirement that the accused believe that their conduct was necessary and reasonable, animations depicted a man pointing a knife at a woman's throat and the woman kicking the man believing she had no choice. In a second contrasting animation, in the same scenario, three other people approached and the man dropped his knife. The woman still kicked him, although it was apparent that alternative action was possible. After hearing or hearing and viewing the instructions, all jurors were tested with a self-defense scenario.

As you can see in figure 5.3, the scores of novice jurors but not legal students improved in the audio-visual (AV) version.

As you look at these results, you can see that the novices were boosted to the same level of understanding as the experts by the addition of visuals to a technical auditory presentation! This experiment extends what we learned about the benefits of adding visuals to text to similar benefits from adding visuals to words presented in audio.

Several experiments that compared the effects of visuals on learning of experts and novices are the basis for my next recommendation.

Figure 5.3. Visuals Lead to Better Jury Understanding of Legal Concepts by Novices but Not Experts

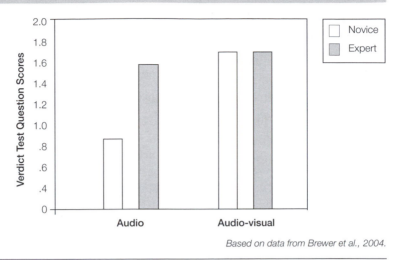

Based on data from Brewer et al., 2004.

♦ ♦ ♦

Graphics Guideline 2:

Emphasize visuals for content novices more than for experienced learners.

♦ ♦ ♦

Beyond the Pumpkin Slide

Imagine you are responsible for updating the sales force on the features of a new printer. Because time is short, you decide to use a show-and-tell architecture delivered through your virtual classroom. With the help of the engineering division you quickly pull together slides that summarize the features of the printer. As you review your first draft, however, it seems pretty boring as most of the slides are text and more text. At this stage you happen to glance at the calendar and realize that it's October, and October means Halloween. Aha! You quickly do a clip art search and find some great jack-o'-lanterns to add to your slides. Yes, your slides do have more eye candy, but what effect, if any, will your last-minute embellishments have on learning?

If you have ever used decorative art to enliven your slides, you are not alone. In an analysis of visuals used in school textbooks, Mayer, Sims, and Tajika (1995) found that pages were about evenly divided between text and illustrations. When they analyzed the type of illustrations used, the overwhelming majority served no useful instructional purpose. In other words, they were pumpkin graphics. In more formal terminology, visuals like these are called *decorative graphics*. Decorative graphics are designed to add visual interest or humor to the material.

Take a look at the visual in figure 5.4 created for a customer service e-learning course.

Figure 5.4. A Photograph Looks Nice on This Screen but Is Irrelevant to the Instructional Content

Gift Certficate Supply Inventory

Types of Supply Inventory

Safe Supply: The gift certificates that are in the safe have been received and accounted for. All safe inventory is accessed by dual control

Counter Supply: The gift certificates that have been accessed outside the safe for daily sales are the counter supply. Counter supply certificates can be accessed by single control.

Used with permission from T+D Magazine.

The lesson developer's organization set a standard that e-learning use only photographs for illustrations. While photographic visuals resulted in a consistent look and feel among the slides, at the same time this standard limited the visual options to support the instructional message.

To improve the potential learning value of the visual, figure 5.5 shows a revision designed to summarize the concepts of safe and counter supplies for gift certificates. While the revised visual may not be as pretty, chances are it will promote learning more effectively.

Can Decorative Visuals Defeat Learning?

You might agree that a decorative visual does not promote learning, but does it really do any harm? Let's see what the evidence tells us. Mayer (2009) evaluated learning from two lessons on how lightning forms. A basic version included text and visuals that illustrated the process of lightning

Figure 5.5. A Revised Graphic Illustrates the Concepts Described in the Text

Used with permission from T+D Magazine.

formation. A spiced up version added some interesting illustrated stories about lightning. For example, a visual of an airplane struck by lightning was accompanied by a brief description of what happens to airplanes struck by lightning. Another visual showed the burns in a football player's uniform caused by a lightning strike. The research team added several illustrated anecdotes like these to the basic lesson on lightning formation. Which version do you think led to better learning? Select the statement(s) that summarize what resulted from this experiment:

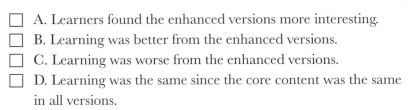

☐ A. Learners found the enhanced versions more interesting.
☐ B. Learning was better from the enhanced versions.
☐ C. Learning was worse from the enhanced versions.
☐ D. Learning was the same since the core content was the same in all versions.

It's true that learners did find the versions with illustrated anecdotes more interesting than the plain Jane versions. Unfortunately, this greater interest did not translate into better learning. Whether presented in a paper-based version or via computer, the basic versions that *omitted* the interesting visuals and stories led to better learning! In five experiments that compared a concise with an embellished version, the high median effect size of 1.66 favored the concise versions. The correct answers to the previous question are A and C.

Decorative Visuals and the Brain

Why do decorative visuals—even visuals related to the topic that generated more interest—defeat learning? Take the example of how lightning forms. Imagine that your brain starts to form an understanding of warm air rising and producing an updraft, then cooling and condensing into a cloud. Then on the next screen, you review some text and visuals about airplanes struck by lightning. Following the airplane story, you see that the top of the cloud extends above the freezing level leading to formation of ice crystals. Next you review some statistics and visuals about the hazards of lightning to golfers. Well, you get the idea. You can see that just as you are building an understanding of lightning formation, you are distracted by interesting but irrelevant content. Because visuals are so powerful, graphics unrelated to your instructional goal at best do not contribute to understanding and at worst actually depress learning!

What Kinds of Visuals Work Best?

If decorative visuals don't help, what kind of visual should you use? Figure 5.6 summarizes four types of explanatory visuals that show relationships among content elements.

Figure 5.6. Four Types of Explanatory Visuals

Type of Visual	Function	Example
Organizational	Shows qualitative relationships among your topics	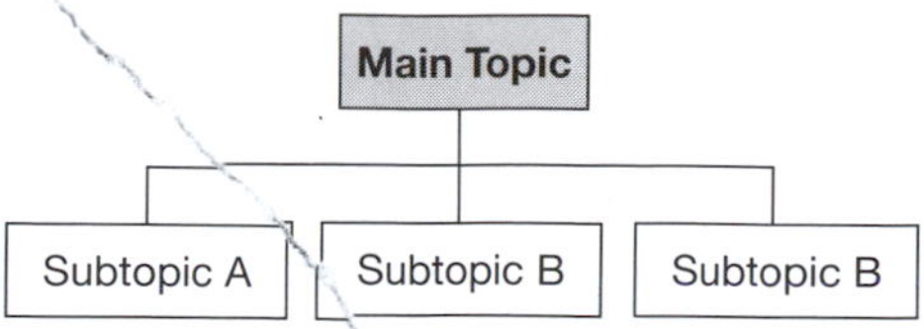
Relational	Shows quantitative relationships in your content	
Transformational	Shows changes in time or space	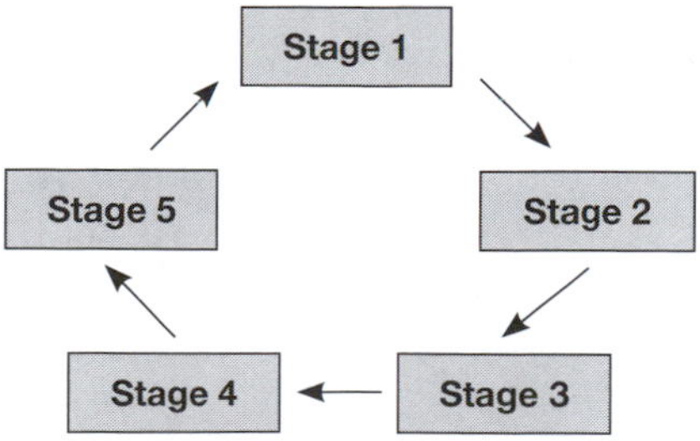
Interpretive	Shows invisible relationships— makes abstract ideas tangible	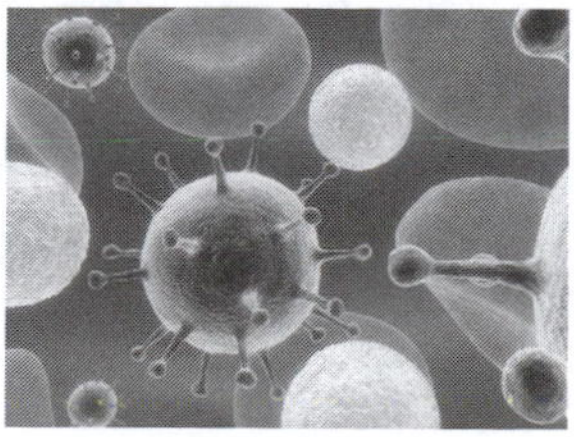

Evidence on learning from different types of visuals is the basis for my third recommendation.

◆ ◆ ◆

Graphics Guideline 3:

Use relevant visuals that depict relationships in your content in lieu of decorative graphics.

◆ ◆ ◆

The Bottom Line

Now that we have summarized key evidence-based guidelines for visuals that best support learning, revisit the questions below and see if you changed any of your ideas from the start of this chapter.

What Do You Think?

Put a check next to each statement about visuals that you believe is true:

☐ A. When you add visuals to text, learning improves.
TRUE. There are, however, some caveats. It's true that visuals have the potential to increase learning, but not all visuals are equally effective.

☐ B. Decorative or thematic visuals increase interest and learning.
FALSE. They may increase interest but do little for learning. That's not to say that you should never use a decorative visual. Just use them judiciously and realize that they will do little to enhance understanding of your content, and in some cases can actually detract from learning.

☐ C. Some learners benefit from visuals more than other learners
TRUE. Some learners do benefit more from visuals than others. However the idea of visual versus auditory learners is a myth. Instead, evidence points to prior knowledge as the most important individual difference linked to learning from visuals. Learners new to your content can be boosted to an expert level with the addition of visuals. Experts, however, won't benefit that much because they can mentally visualize the content just by reading or hearing

the words. Therefore, invest your visual resources primarily in foundational lessons designed for learners new to your content.

☐ D. Not all visuals are equally effective.
TRUE. Based on analysis of options A and B, this is a true statement.

Applying Visuals to Your Training

Whether you are using slides in the classroom or preparing screens for e-learning, visuals can be one of your most powerful teaching allies. Although you will need to invest more time and effort compared to producing materials that consist of mostly words, when your learners are new to the content and when your goal is meaningful learning, we have ample evidence for a return-on-investment in relevant graphics.

Consider the following questions as you review your content:

☐ What relationships are important in my lesson?
☐ Which explanatory visuals can I use to reinforce those relationships?
☐ Do I have multiple topics that could benefit from an organizational graphic such as a flow chart, table, or tree diagram?
☐ Am I trying to illustrate a process or procedure that involves changes over time and could benefit from some type of transformational visual?
☐ Does my lesson include abstract ideas or concepts? If so, can I use a visual analogy to create an interpretive visual?
☐ Have I included visuals that will distract from the learning goal? If yes, either delete or move those visuals out of the body of the lesson.

Most trainers have historically worked primarily in text. Therefore, you may need to prime your pump to think visually as follows:

☐ Start a collection of images, especially explanatory images that effectively communicate ideas. Remember that most images are copyrighted. The goal of your collection, however, is not the use the images you find but to consider how the visual techniques can be adapted to your own goals.

☐ Use your cell phone or digital camera to capture images as you do your job analysis. For example, take snapshots of sketches that subject matter experts make when explaining their ideas. Take photos of equipment or work-relevant settings.

☐ Check out your organization's resources. You might be lucky to have access to a graphic artist who can help you translate your ideas into images. You might have a corporate repository of work-relevant images that you can repurpose into your lesson.

For More Information

Clark, R.C., & C. Lyons (in press). *Graphics for Learning*, 2d ed. San Francisco: Pfeiffer.

Brewer, N., S. Harvey, & C. Semmler (2004). "Improving comprehension of jury instructions with audio-visual presentation." *Applied Cognitive Psychology* 18, 765–76.

Butcher, K.R. (2006). "Learning from text with diagrams: Promoting mental model development and inference generation." *Journal of Educational Psychology* 98(1): 182–97.

Mayer, R.E. (2009). *Multimedia Learning*, 2d ed. New York: Cambridge University Press. See chs. 4 and 12.

◆ ◆ ◆

Explain Visuals

The Power of Explanations

What Are Explanations?

Should You Explain Visuals with Text, Audio, or Both?

Explaining Visuals with Text and Audio

Explanations and the Brain

Explaining Visuals with Text

The Bottom Line

Applying Explanations to Your Training

◆ ◆ ◆

Chapter 6

Explain Visuals

Imagine that you have lined up a set of visuals for your lesson. You have identified some screen captures to illustrate a computer procedure. Next you need to write the words to describe the actions in the visuals. Many trainers believe that words placed in text plus audio narration of those words accommodates different learning styles as well as learners with visual or auditory disabilities.

by Ann Kwinn & C. Kwinn

What is the best way to explain on-screen visuals, either in e-learning or in the classroom?

In this chapter we will look at the evidence for how to maximize the learning value of words you use to explain visuals.

The Power of Explanations

We've seen in chapter 5 that relevant visuals can dramatically improve learning. However, most visuals are *not* self-explanatory. For meaningful learning, you need both visuals and words to communicate your content. You need to decide whether to present words in audio, text, or both text and audio. If you decide to use text, you need to decide where to place the text in conjunction with the visuals. For example, should you place it at the bottom or on the side of each slide to be consistent? Or should you place the text into the visual? Or does it matter where you place text?

What Do You Think?

Look at the examples in figures 6.1, 6.2, 6.3, and 6.4. The content is basically the same in all of the examples. What varies is how and where words are presented.

Figure 6.1. Use of Words to Explain a Visual—Version A

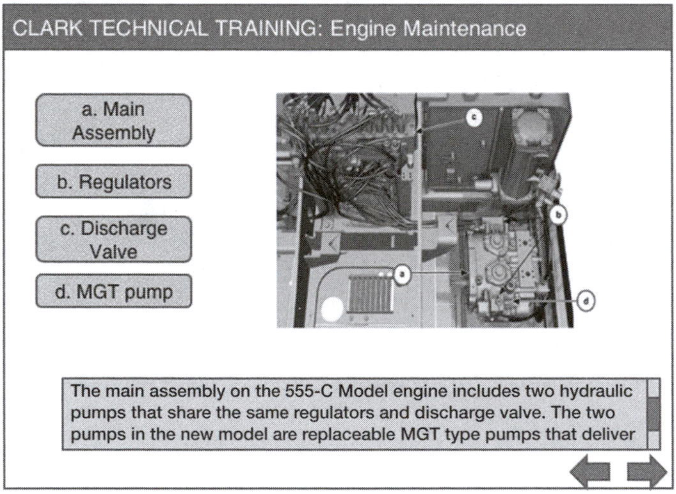

CLARK TECHNICAL TRAINING: Engine Maintenance

a. Main Assembly

b. Regulators

c. Discharge Valve

d. MGT pump

The main assembly on the 555-C Model engine includes two hydraulic pumps that share the same regulators and discharge valve. The two pumps in the new model are replaceable MGT type pumps that deliver

Figure 6.2. Use of Words to Explain a Visual—Version B

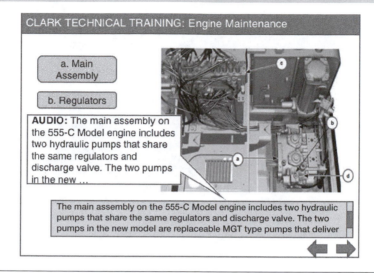

Figure 6.3. Use of Words to Explain a Visual—Version C

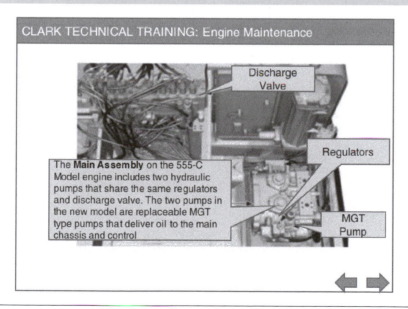

Figure 6.4. Use of Words to Explain a Visual—Version D

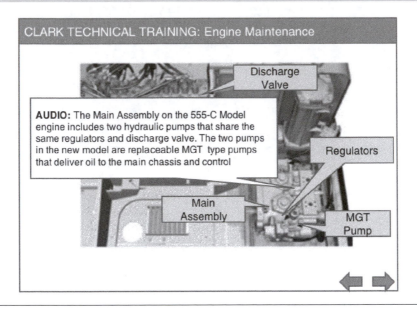

After you review these four treatments, check which presentation of words is best for learning:

- ☐ Version A in figure 6.1 because the layout is the cleanest.
- ☐ Version B in figure 6.2 because the explanations are presented in text and in audio narration of that text.
- ☐ Version C in figure 6.3 because it uses only text placed in the visual.
- ☐ Version D in figure 6.4 since the explanations are presented primarily in audio.

In this chapter I will review evidence that addresses these issues and give you guidance on the best ways to leverage words used to explain visuals.

What Are Explanations?

For the purpose of this chapter I focus primarily on words used to explain visuals. The words may be presented in text and/or in audio narration. The combination of the visual and the words should support the learning objective. For example, when teaching a procedure, your demonstration uses words to describe the actions illustrated in the visuals. When teaching a principle such as how to defuse a tense customer situation, you debrief a video example with words. When teaching a business process such as the performance appraisal cycle, you explain a cycle chart with words. When explaining about the parts of equipment as in Figures 6.1 to 6.4 you use words to label the equipment and to explain how it works. In all of these instances, the combination of a relevant visual with words in text or in audio or both are used to communicate the content.

Should You Explain Visuals with Text, Audio, or Both?

As I discussed in chapter 1, it's a common misconception that some learners are visual learners while others are auditory learners and therefore we need to support both styles by presenting words in text as well as narration. For example, the screen shown in figure 6.2 describes the equipment with text plus audio of that text. If the lesson is delivered by computer such as figure 6.2, the text would appear on the screen and the audio would be delivered through narration. If the lesson is delivered in a classroom, the text would appear on the slide and the instructor would provide a verbal explanation. Is this a good idea or would learning be better if you used only text or only audio to describe the visual? Fortunately, we have evidence to guide your choice of modalities to present words.

Evidence on Text Versus Audio Explanations

Many experiments have compared learning from visuals explained by words in audio with learning from visuals explained by the same words in text. In fact, enough of these studies have been done to allow a meta-analysis (Ginns 2005) as well as a less formal review of several experiments (Moreno 2006). The experimental lessons included in the meta-analysis involved various types of content including mathematics, electrical engineering, environmental science, and explanations of how brakes and lightning work. The meta-analysis reported that learning was consistently better when visuals were *explained by audio narration* with a high effect size of

.72. This means that if a lesson that used text to explain visuals resulted in an average score of 70 percent with a standard deviation of 8, the same lesson that used audio would yield an average score of about 76 percent. The variety and amount of evidence on the use of audio gives me a high degree of confidence in my first recommendation.

◆ ◆ ◆

Explanation Guideline 1:

Explain visuals with audio narration rather than text to maximize learning.

◆ ◆ ◆

When teaching in the classroom, incorporate relevant visuals on your slides and explain them with a verbal instructor explanation. When teaching via self-study e-learning, place relevant visuals on the screens and explain them with audio narration. Figure 6.5 shows the visual treatment we discussed in chapter 5 in the lesson on Gift Certificate Supply Inventory (see figure 5.6). In this version however, I have replaced all of the onscreen text with audio narration.

Figure 6.5. Audio is Used to Explain a Visual

Used with permission from T+D *Magazine.*

Manage Mental Load When Using Audio

A drawback to audio is its transience. In e-learning always incorporate play controls to allow learners to stop and replay the audio. In addition, keep your audio explanations lean. Learners get impatient with lengthy audio segments.

Explaining Visuals with Text and Audio

As I mentioned previously, it's common practice to explain a visual with words in text and audio narration of that text to accommodate different learning styles or to be compliant with requirements for learners with visual or auditory disabilities. We have, however, quite a bit of evidence proving that learning is depressed when you deliver the same words in both text and audio! Experiments compared learning from lessons in which visuals were explained with audio alone as illustrated in figure 6.4 with lessons in which visuals were explained with audio *plus* onscreen text that repeats the words in the audio narration as illustrated in figure 6.2. The results? Learners in the *audio-alone lessons* scored higher with a median effect size of .72, which is considered large (Mayer 2009). The ample evidence we have from many experiments is the basis for my second recommendation.

◆ ◆ ◆

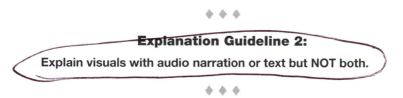

Explanation Guideline 2:
Explain visuals with audio narration or text but NOT both.

◆ ◆ ◆

How can you apply this principle *and* accommodate learners with disabilities? I recommend that as a default, you explain a visual with audio in the form of narration in e-learning *or* as instructor explanations in the classroom. At the same time, provide an option for hearing impaired. In e-learning you can include an audio control icon. When audio is turned off, onscreen text appears. In synchronous e-learning, use closed captioning. In a classroom, sign language or a handout with slides and text can augment the instructor's presentation.

Explanations and the Brain

We saw in chapter 2, that working memory has two processing centers: one for auditory information and one for visual. As summarized in figure 6.6, when you explain a complex visual with text, all of the information bombards the visual center. In contrast, as shown in figure 6.7, when you explain a complex visual with audio, you divide the load between the visual and the auditory centers. In this way, you maximize the limited capacity of working memory to process information.

Figure 6.6. Text and Visuals Can Overload Visual Center in Memory

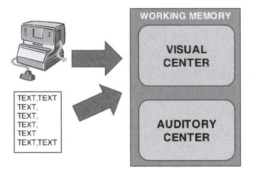

Figure 6.7. Use of Narration to Explain Visuals Balances Content in Memory

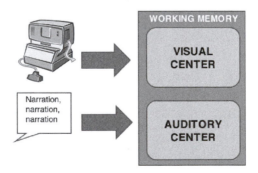

Synchronization of text and narration can be the source of a second problem with simultaneous text and audio narration of that text. Each of us reads at our own rate, which in turn is different from the rate of the narrator. Trying to synchronize our own reading rate with that of the narrator just adds unnecessary mental overhead. To compensate, most of us either ignore the text and listen to the narration or turn off the narration and read the text. The bottom line is this: Use audio to explain complex visuals and avoid a combination of text and redundant narration of that text.

So what about audio and visual learning styles? The reality is that we are all visual learners—that is, we can all profit from a relevant visual when learning unfamiliar knowledge and skills. Furthermore, we are all auditory learners—that is, we can all benefit when a complex visual is described by audio narration rather than overloading our visual center with text.

Exceptions to the Rule on Use of Audio to Explain Visuals

The reason audio is generally more effective than text to explain a complex visual is because it reduces mental load. There are some situations, however, when using audio would actually increase mental load, and these give rise to exceptions to the rule:

1. *Language issues.* If you have studied a foreign language you know that listening is a challenging skill—more than reading which you can do at your own rate. Therefore, for individuals who are not native speakers in the language of the training, present words in text.

2. *No visuals.* When there are no visuals or the visuals are very simple, the visual center is not as likely to be overloaded.

3. *Experienced learners.* More advanced learners are probably better off moving at their own pace by reading text and bypassing explanations that are not relevant to them. Because they have quite a bit

of content background, they can be trusted to make good decisions about what they do and do not need.

4. *New terms.* When new technical terms, data, or content such as formulas are presented, learners benefit from seeing and hearing those terms. Use text and audio to present these new terms.

5. *Reference content.* Any content that learners will need to refer back to periodically such as directions to exercises or case study data would be better placed in text because audio is transient.

What About Bulleted Text?

It's a common practice on either slides or e-learning screens to place a visual on half of the screen and on the other half to place some concise text phrases usually in bullet points. The instructor then elaborates on the bullet points with additional words. Does this practice impede learning?

Mayer and Johnson (2008) compared learning from lessons in which visuals were explained with audio alone to the same lesson that added brief text captions drawn from the narration. Learning was equal from both versions. Based on this finding, you should get about the same learning from an audio-alone version as from an audio-plus-brief-captions version as shown in figure 6.8.

Explaining Visuals with Text

Sometimes, however, you must use text to explain your visuals. Books, for example, can't carry audio. Some e-learning courses avoid audio due to bandwidth, lack of headsets, or other technical issues. When you present explanations of visuals with text, where should you position the text? For example, it could be put at the bottom of the screen as in figure 6.1. Alternatively, it could be integrated into the visual as in figure 6.3. Does the placement of text matter?

Have you ever been reading a book and found that an important diagram is located on the *back* of the page describing that diagram? To get a full understanding, you need to flip back and forth to read the text and then

Figure 6.8. Use of Narration and Text Bullets to Explain a Visual

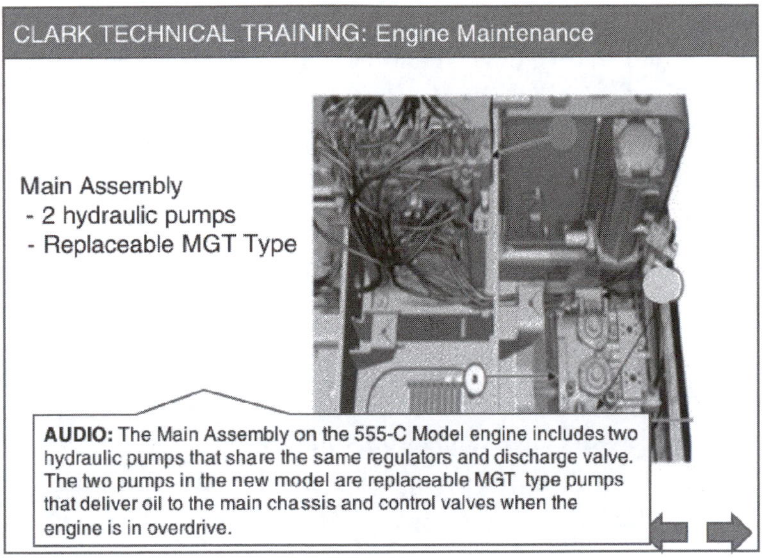

CLARK TECHNICAL TRAINING: Engine Maintenance

Main Assembly
- 2 hydraulic pumps
- Replaceable MGT Type

AUDIO: The Main Assembly on the 555-C Model engine includes two hydraulic pumps that share the same regulators and discharge valve. The two pumps in the new model are replaceable MGT type pumps that deliver oil to the main chassis and control valves when the engine is in overdrive.

review the visual. How does that make you feel? Most of us find this an annoying experience! That annoyance is actually your working memory complaining about the extra burden of having to hold content in its limited space while viewing related content and trying to integrate both elements. And this experience is not just your imagination. Researchers have measured learning from layouts like the examples in figures 6.1 and 6.3. Mayer (2009) reported that in five out of five experiments, learners studying from lessons that used integrated text learned more than those studying lessons with separated text. The median effect size is about 1, which indicates high practical significance. Experiments like these are the basis for my third explanations principle.

❖ ❖ ❖

Explanation Guideline 3:

When using text to explain a visual, place the text close by the relevant part of the visual.

❖ ❖ ❖

There are many common violations of this simple principle in all delivery media. For example, in e-learning, a scrolling page shows a visual at the top of the page and the text underneath the visual. When you view the visual you can't see the text and vice versa. On a paper job aid, text that describes a procedure is placed under the illustration. A better solution is to insert text captions right into the relevant portion of the visual. Another common violation is to split an exercise between a workbook and a computer application. The learner reads the steps or the data in the workbook and tries to apply them on the computer. A better solution is to include all of the steps on the computer.

Whether you are using books, computers, or job aids to deliver your training, separating text and related diagrams leads to split attention and imposes unnecessary mental load on your learners. Mayer (2009, 145) summarizes the problem: "The format of much instruction is determined by tradition, economic factors, or the whim of the instructor. Cognitive factors are rarely considered resulting in instructional designs in which split attention is common."

That said, I'm hoping you won't experience too many instances of separated text and visuals in this book. In all of my books I have found that publisher templates often place text on one page and the relevant visual on the back of that page. It would be much better if some figures could be reduced in size and placed on one side of a page with text wrap. Customization of layouts, however, incurs additional cost and as a result is rare. As an author, I have worked with publishers to minimize split text and visuals by editing out text or eliminating figures so that the remaining text and figures end up on the same page spread. I mention all of this not just to make excuses but to illustrate how practical realities such as the limitations of your delivery media or budget or time will shape your products. Evidence is never the only factor to be considered in design and development of instructional environments!

The Bottom Line

What Do You Think?

Based on figures 6.1–6.4, you indicated which versions were best for learning. Below are my comments.

☐ Version A in figure 6.1, because the layout is the cleanest.
Option A is likely to lead to split attention because two different text segments are displayed separately from the visual. It is not best for learning.

☐ Version B in figure 6.2, because the explanations are presented in text and in audio narration of that text.
This option would prove to be the worst treatment for learning. We have seen evidence that learning is depressed when explanations are presented in text and audio narration of that text. In addition, the onscreen text is placed at the bottom of the screen leading to split attention.

☐ Version C in figure 6.3 is best for learning, because it uses only text placed in the visual.
If audio is not an option, this example is the most effective because the text is integrated into the figure.

☐ Version D in figure 6.4, because the explanations are presented primarily in audio.
This version is the most effective because it uses audio narration to describe a complex visual. It also displays new technical terms in text on the screen.

Applying Explanations to Your Training

Regardless of your delivery environment, you will generally need words to explain your visuals. Apply the following guidelines to maximize learning from those words:

If your delivery environment supports audio,

☐ use audio narration alone to describe a large visual on the screen
☐ use audio narration plus a few words in text taken from the narration placed in bullet points nearby the visual
☐ avoid using text sentences and narration of those sentences to explain a visual.

The use of audio to describe visuals is *not* recommended under the following conditions:

- ☐ Learners are not native speakers.
- ☐ New technical terms are introduced.
- ☐ Learners need to refer back to the words.
- ☐ There are no visuals on the screen or slide.
- ☐ Your learners are experienced and not likely to be overloaded.

If your delivery environment does not support audio,

- ☐ enlarge the visual on the slide and integrate text into the visual
- ☐ use callouts to place multiple text statements nearby relevant portions of the visual.

In the next chapter we will continue our discussion of explanations by showing how you can maximize learning by exploiting human social instincts.

For More Information

Clark, R.C., & R.E. Mayer (2008b). *e-Learning & the Science of Instruction*, 2d ed. San Francisco: Pfeiffer. See chs. 4, 5, and 6.

Mayer, R.E. (2009). *Multimedia Learning*, 2d ed. New York: Cambridge University Press. See chs. 6, 7, and 11.

◆ ◆ ◆

Make It Personal

◆ ◆ ◆

Chapter 7

Make It Personal

Facebook, Twitter, MySpace, LinkedIn are all examples of member communities that in only a few years have become the world's fourth most popular online sector after search, portals, and PC software applications. Facebook alone, with over 300 million unique monthly visitors as of third quarter 2009, draws double the traffic of any of the "big four" portals, including Google. The explosion of social media reflects our ancient imperative: human to human communication. How can training environments leverage social presence to improve learning?

by Ann Kwinn & C. Kwinn

In this chapter we will look at proven methods to leverage social presence—not through social media but through even more basic devices such as speaking directly to your learners in your explanations, using online agents, and leveraging the power of the human voice.

Leveraging Social Presence

I gave a keynote speech recently during which I discussed the research on the effects of music on learning. Many in the audience were online, engaged no doubt in a multitude of activities that did not involve my presentation. However, one participant sent out some tweets about music and learning and told our group that within a space of five minutes she received about 100 responses. She was excited about the instant extension of my presentation into an immediate and lively virtual discussion.

I confess to mixed feelings. While it was nice that my presentation was extended in real time to a much larger audience, I wondered whether participants busy tweeting about music and learning (or any other topics of interest) missed my next five or six key points.

Like all technology applications, social media is a mixed blessing. Responding to low productivity of their workforce, for example, several Italian companies have blocked access to Facebook (Nielsen Report 2009). But I digress. This chapter is not about social media per se. Rather it's about more fundamental methods trainers can use to leverage social presence in ways proven to improve learning.

One of the unique products of human evolution is our universal sociability. It grew from the need to cooperate to survive. Cooperation relies fundamentally on communication: listening, processing, and responding to our social partners to achieve mutual goals. So, embedded is this instinctive response that even self-study e-learning that projects human persona can command our attention. We know in our heads that the computer is inanimate. But we are unwittingly compelled to process information more deeply when it embeds social cues. This is what we mean by *social presence*.

In this chapter we will look at several techniques you can use in the classroom, in workbooks, or in e-learning to exploit human processing of social cues in ways that optimize learning. In particular we will look at techniques to optimize explanations and consider the role of the instructor's image and the instructor's voice to promote social presence.

What Do You Think?

The content in the e-learning screens in figures 7.1 and 7.2 is similar. However, they differ regarding social presence. Compare them and put a check by the statements you think are true.

Figure 7.1. Version A of an Excel Lesson

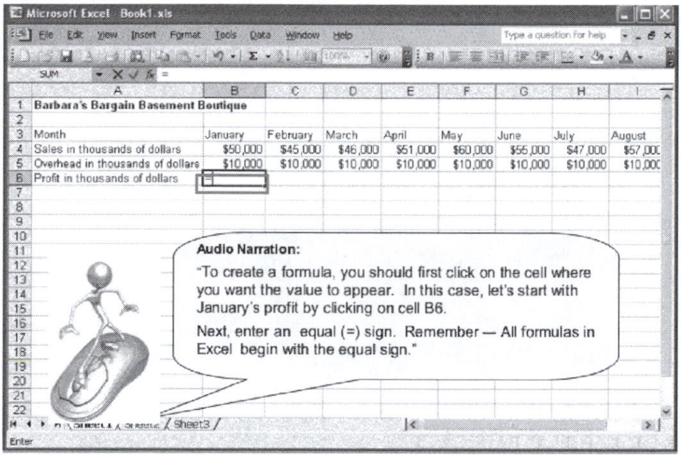

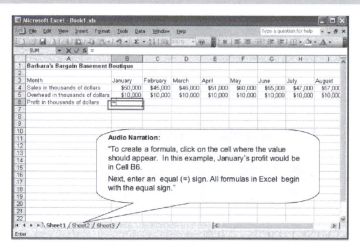

Figure 7.2. Version B of an Excel Lesson

☐ Version A will lead to better learning than Version B.

☐ Version B will lead to better learning than Version A.

☐ Versions A and B will lead to equivalent learning since the content is the same.

Both screens include instructional visuals and instructional words. Version A projects a more conversational tone primarily through the use of first- and second-person pronouns, polite language as well as an onscreen virtual tutor. Version B is a bit more formal and does not include an onscreen agent. You might feel that version B is more business like and projects greater credibility. Alternatively, you might feel that the more casual tone in version A will lead to increased attention. In this chapter we will look at the evidence and psychology for how learning is affected by social cues such as first- and second-person language, personable instructors, and onscreen agents.

What Is Personalized Training?

By *personalized training* I refer to instructional environments that embed social cues. Social cues can take the form of

- first- and second-person rather than third-person language
- polite phrases
- instructor images or avatars in e-learning
- voice quality of e-learning narration
- instructors as hosts
- social interactions such as collaborative problem solving during training sessions.

Lectures in a large classroom setting can be delivered in a traditional academic manner with minimal interaction between learners and instructor or among learners. Alternatively, instructors can create a more intimate environment through their tone, through self-revelation, through body language, and by including some collaborative exercises during the session. Personalized training increases social presence. Is learning better in environments with high social presence? If so, which techniques have proven most effective? These are the questions we will consider in this chapter.

Course Ratings and Social Presence

It's common practice at the end of a training session to ask participants to rate the quality of the instruction. Typical questions ask about learner perception of the instructor and the learning environment. Researchers have studied the relationship between student ratings and various features of the learning environment. A meta-analysis that included over 27,000 student ratings reported three main factors in the training environment associated with higher student ratings: 1) motivation to attend the training, 2) instructor style, and 3) social presence during learning (Sitzmann et al. 2008).

Regarding instructor style, trainers who were psychologically "available" to learners and who projected a relaxed friendly persona were associated with higher learner satisfaction ratings. In addition, opportunities to engage with other class members during the learning event were also correlated with higher ratings. Although higher class ratings don't necessarily translate into more learning, by including social cues proven to increase learning, you can get better course ratings *and* better learning outcomes. The evidence on course ratings is the basis for my first guideline.

◆ ◆ ◆

Personalization Guideline 1:

Get higher course ratings by incorporating social presence into your learning event.

◆ ◆ ◆

Personalization and the Brain

How does personalization promote deeper learning? The key lies in the greater attention and mental effort we invest in social messages compared to messages lacking social cues. Attending to and deeply processing interpersonal messages likely evolved from eons in which survival depended on mutual cooperation. Your brain is tuned to social cues and unconsciously devotes more attention and mental effort to processing associated social messages. More attention and deeper processing in working memory lead to a higher probability of encoding associated content into long-term memory.

I contrast my own mental state when watching TV, attending a keynote speech at a conference, and conversing with a colleague. TV often gets only cursory attention and rather shallow processing. In fact for many, TV is a route to relaxation due to its soporific effects. A keynote speech may generate a bit more attention, especially if the delivery techniques are effective and content is relevant. Even here, however, I often find my mind wandering. Sometimes the speech sends me down my own thought rabbit trail. Other times I tune out completely because I know the speaker will not expect any response from me. However, when conversing with others either in a small group or one on one, my level of attention and processing investment is higher because of mutual satisfaction and unspoken agreements of social participation.

Is Conversational Language Better Than Formal Language?

Compare the introductions to a botany simulation game in figure 7.3 What differences do you see? Which do you think would lead to better learning?

Figure 7.3. Two Introductions to a Botany Game

Version A

This program is about what type of plant survives on different planets. For each planet, a plant will be designed. The goal is to learn what type of roots, stem, and leaves allow plants to survive in each environment.

Version B

You are about to start on a journey where you will be visiting different planets. For each planet, you will need to design a plant. Your mission is to learn what type of roots, stem, and leaves will allow your plant to survive in each environment.

From Mayer (2009), p. 246.

In a series of experiments in which the words were delivered either by text or by audio narration, the more conversational versions (text or audio) that used first- and second-person language resulted in more learning! In 11 experimental lessons that used different content and compared learning from first- and second-person language with learning from third-person constructions, all studies favored use of first and second person (Mayer 2009). All of the lessons were delivered by computer. Some were standard online tutorials and some were games. The effect sizes ranged from .52 to 1.93 for a median of 1.11. That means that on average you could expect a one standard deviation improvement in lessons that speak directly to the learners using "I" and "you" statements. Although all of these lessons were computer delivered, it is likely that the same benefits would accrue from lessons in workbooks or classroom training. We need additional research to confirm the universal effectiveness of this technique that includes different types of content and also considers cultural differences in learner populations.

Politeness Pays

A recent study by Wang et al. (2008) compared two versions of a lesson focusing on engineering problems through a one-hour computer game called Virtual Factory. The game included a virtual tutor who made suggestions and gave feedback in either a directive or polite manner. For example, in the direct wording version the tutor might say: "Save the factory now" rather than "Do you want to save the factory now?" The more polite version resulted in better learning.

Based on strong and consistent evidence to date, I recommend the following.

◆ ◆ ◆

Personalization Guideline 2:

Promote deeper learning by speaking in a conversational manner using first and second person and polite phrases.

◆ ◆ ◆

Instructors as Learning Hosts

In many learning environments such as books, online computer lessons or even traditional classroom settings, the author or instructor remain aloof from the learners. They stick to their content and don't make any self-revelations such as how they may personally feel about the content or specific experiences they have had related to the lesson content. Imagine reading a text on parasitology in which the author scientifically explains the adverse effects of various parasites including how they access their host organisms. Now imagine reading a similar passage in which the author describes a time he was infected even though he was very careful with what he ate and drank. He found that the hotel housekeeping staff rinsed the ash trays in the toilet and he had laid his cigarette on such an ash tray. Stories are very memorable and must be used carefully to promote the instructional goal. A relevant personal narrative can improve learning by generating attention and increasing social presence. This parasite story was told to my biology class over 40 years ago. I don't recall the instructor or her name. But I do remember the story!

In addition to stories, the injection of personal opinion or reactions to content has been shown to improve learning. For example, an instructor might present two views on an issue and reveal his or her own personal opinion. Mayer (2009) refers to self-revealing episodes as a *visible author* technique. He describes several research comparisons that favored learning from the visible author.

Whether writing for a textbook, writing for e-learning, or preparing lecture notes for a face-to-face class, instructors can improve learning by thinking of themselves as a *learning host*. Good hosts make their guests feel comfortable and engage them in the event. They make themselves available both physically and emotionally to their guests. In face-to-face environments, good instructors project accessibility by how they dress, how they greet learners, and by using diverse social cues to set an informal but productive tone throughout the event. In a similar manner, when authoring texts or e-learning courses, use hosting techniques proven to increase learning and generate better student ratings.

Student ratings and learning evidence are the basis for my third recommendation.

◆ ◆ ◆

Personalization Guideline 3:

When communicating instructional content in texts, on computer, or in the classroom, adopt hosting techniques by using appropriate social cues that make you accessible to your learners.

◆ ◆ ◆

As a footnote, as I mentioned in chapter 1, much of the research I've discussed was conducted with U.S. learners, mostly of a college age. Other cultures and other generations might respond to different cues—cues that are considered the social norm. Although I have found that workshop participants in the United States are 99 percent receptive to collaborative activities, group discussions in a workshop I led in Norway were not well received. They felt I was the expert, and they did not want to "waste" their time listening to their colleagues. We will need additional research to see how findings regarding social presence apply to diverse settings.

Do Onscreen Agents or Instructor Images Improve Learning?

In a face-to-face classroom, the instructor's persona pretty much dictates the image and voice. In both synchronous and asynchronous e-learning, however, you can decide to incorporate an instructor's video image, use an avatar (an online character) image, or include no image at all. Figure 7.4 shows a screen shot from an online class that includes the image of the instructor through use of a webcam. Similarly, in asynchronous e-learning, you can use an online tutor in the form of an onscreen tutor as shown in figure 7.1. What evidence do we have for the benefits of instructor images in e-learning?

Mayer (2009) tested several different images added to an online botany game. These included a cartoon character called Herman the Bug and

Figure 7.4. The Instructor Uses the Webcam to Project Her Image During a Webinar

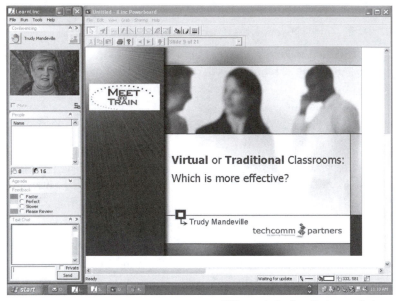

With permission from Techcomm Partners.

a human "talking head" video. He reports that merely adding the speaker's image to the screen did not produce strong or consistent learning improvement. However, perhaps if an onscreen character served some instructionally useful purpose such as to point to an important part of a visual, learning would be better. In fact, Lusk and Atkinson (2007) improved learning from an online agent that used gestures to draw attention to important content on the screen compared to a static onscreen avatar that offered no more benefit than a lesson with no avatar. Be careful, however! Simply adding the instructor's image may lead to split attention—distracting the focus from important visual and textual elements on the screen.

I have taught many synchronous virtual classes and have avoided the use of a webcam—mostly because it was technically easier and besides I didn't need to comb my hair or put on makeup. I'm glad to see there is some evidence to support my lack of enthusiasm for the webcam. Based on evidence to date, I offer my next recommendation.

◆ ◆ ◆

Personalization Guideline 4:

Use care with instructor images on the screen in e-learning. Be sure the avatar serves some useful instructional role.

◆ ◆ ◆

As an exception to this guideline, I don't think it does any harm to include an instructor image during the introductory segments of a lesson. Afterward, however, the image does not add anything and may become a distraction.

Does Voice Quality Matter?

In contrast to the instructor's image, evidence does suggest you give consideration to the voice used in audio narration. In comparing a narration given by a native English speaker using a friendly tone with the same narration from a high quality speech synthesizer, learning was much better from the human voice version. Learners may also be sensitive to different accents and voice quality such as a male or female voice. We don't have much research on this although one study showed better learning among American students from a generic American-accented voice compared to a Russian-accented voice (Mayer 2009). It may be that learners more deeply process messages that sound like they come from someone like them in terms of gender, race, or ethnic identity. Many questions remain. Are there cultural differences? Are some accents better received than others? Does the content make a difference? We will need more evidence to refine our guidelines regarding audio narration.

Does Collaboration Improve Learning?

As I mentioned at the start of this chapter, classes that incorporate opportunities for learners to engage with one another as well as with the instructor get higher student ratings than classes that minimize social engagement. I use different types of *collaborative learning* exercises in my face-to-face workshops as well as in the virtual classroom. In my workshop *e-Learning and the Science of Instruction,* I use a collaborative technique called Jigsaw. Each participant is assigned one of 10 chapters to review. Then each participant meets with others who read the same chapter to create a teaching aid. Chapter teams then summarize their chapter to the entire class using their teaching aid. In addition to Jigsaw teams, I form different case study teams to apply the guidelines learned from the chapter presentations to an e-learning case study. Group techniques like these are common in classroom and virtual classroom events. Asynchronous distance learning may inject collaborative assignments via discussion boards, social networking sites, and email. What evidence do we have for the learning benefits of collaboration?

Unfortunately, results from many studies comparing collaborative with solo learning have been mixed due to many differences among collaborative learning methods such as group size, structure of the group assignment, composition of the groups, and learning outcomes, among others. This is another example of the "No Yellow Brick Road Effect" I mentioned in chapter 1. If you are interested in the details of this research, take a look at chapter 12 in *e-Learning & the Science of Instruction.*

I believe that the major value of collaborative learning lies in the potential of prompting learners to process content more deeply than if they reviewed the material on their own.

An Experimental Comparison of Individual and Collaborative Learning

Krause, Stark, and Mandl (2009) compared learning of statistics principles from individual and collaborative e-learning. Learners completed an online statistics lesson either individually or in groups of two. The small teams performed better during the instructional phase than solo students. In other words, the problem solutions from teams were better than the solutions from individuals. However, this better team performance on practice problems did not pay off in individual learning. On the posttest, there were no differences between those who worked alone and those who worked together. The authors concluded that "cooperative learning did not affect objective learning outcomes . . . all the same, cooperation did not impair learning" (167).

In contrast, Barab and her colleagues (2009) reported better problem-solving learning (although not concept learning) from pairs who worked through a virtual world lesson than individuals working through the same lesson on their own. We have much to learn about the best conditions for collaborative learning.

How I Use Collaboration

As I mentioned, I routinely use various forms of collaborative learning in my workshops. Here is a summary of my own lessons learned. To start, the assignment needs to be manageable. Too simple, and there is not enough challenge to motivate team work. Too complex, and groups get frustrated and run out of time. I usually find when piloting a new team case assignment that I need to simplify it. Clear assignment directions are important. I've found that groups tend to get more confused than individuals when interpreting an assignment. I often augment the directions with some examples of the deliverables. The size of the group also makes a difference. I have found best results with smaller groups ranging from two to four depending on the time frame and assignment. Consistent with the research I described at the start of this chapter, I find most learners in the United States at least rate an event higher when some social interactions are incorporated. You will need to consider a variety of factors when deciding how, when, and where to incorporate collaborative learning into your learning events. At this point, I don't see sufficient consistent research evidence to offer any guiding principles.

A Postscript on Social Media

I started the chapter mentioning the rocketing popularity of social media. At this point in time, I have not seen controlled research on the use of social media to improve learning. However, based on over 60 years of media research as well as the evidence on collaborative learning, I can make some educated guesses. The benefits of social media will depend on how the applications are used to support learning and knowledge management. To the extent that they support human memory processes and are congruent with learning goals, social media should provide yet another tool to extend learning by leveraging social presence. From my perspective, that means these tools should be applied in focused and deliberate ways that do not split attention and that do promote deeper processing of content.

The Bottom Line

What Do You Think?

We started with two samples from an e-learning course. Review those samples and see if your answers below have changed.

- ☐ Version A will lead to better learning than version B.
- ☐ Version B will lead to better learning than version A.
- ☐ Versions A and B will lead to equivalent learning because the content is the same.

Based on evidence to date, I recommend version A because it incorporates more social cues that should lead to better learning. But the main element that makes it more effective is the use of first- and second-person conversational language and not the virtual tutor. We need more research on onscreen agents to define whether and how their use can contribute to learning.

Applying Personalization to Your Training

Whether you are working in a classroom or online, leverage human instincts to deeply process social information. In the classroom you can get higher student ratings and improve learning by making yourself psychologically accessible to your learners. In other words, dress and act in a manner that will make your audience feel comfortable. Note that there may be cultural differences in how you implement this principle. In most Western cultures you should greet your learners individually, use eye contact, maintain appropriate physical proximity to your learners, speak in a conversational tone, encourage and respond to comments and questions, and incorporate some collaborative activities when and where appropriate.

In synchronous e-learning, you need not use the webcam although you may want to include a video or still shot of yourself at the start of the session. As in a physical classroom, you should speak with your learners individually, invite learners to use audio when practical, use a relaxed and conversational tone and reveal your own experiences and opinions on the content.

In asynchronous e-learning or books you have fewer tools for social presence. Most important will be text (or audio scripts) that use the first and second person, a conversational polite tone, and a voice quality familiar to your target audience. I offer the following checklist as a summary guide:

- ☐ Use first- and second-person language in your explanations.
- ☐ Use a polite conversational tone.
- ☐ Offer your own relevant experiences and perspectives on the content.
- ☐ Offer relevant opportunities for social engagement among your participants.
- ☐ Use care adding an onscreen image of the instructor in e-learning. Be sure the avatar plays an instructional role and is not distracting.
- ☐ Use a friendly voice for narration. Avoid narration that may seem unnatural to your learners.

For More Information

Clark, R.C., & R.E. Mayer (2008b). *e-Learning & the Science of Instruction*, 2d ed. San Francisco: Pfeiffer. See chs. 8 and 12.

Mayer, R.E. (2009). *Multimedia Learning*, 2d ed. New York: Cambridge University Press. See ch. 13.

◆ ◆ ◆

Avoid Too Much of a Good Thing

◆ ◆ ◆

Chapter 8

Avoid Too Much of a Good Thing

I watched a movie recently that was definitely too much of a good thing. It was called *Australia* and if you missed it, don't worry. The plot was a bit time-worn but the scenery was nice and I was hanging in as the heroine foiled the bad guys and saved her ranch. As the hero and heroine embraced, I waited for the requisite sunset and credits. But the movie was only half over. It went on to spin out a whole new plot that consumed another hour and a half, leaving me to wonder: Where was the editor?

by Ann Kwinn & C. Kwinn

I've been guilty of the same type of excess when writing a book or giving a presentation—too many chapters, too much detail in a chapter, too many slides, too many topics.

This is a chapter about resisting the urge to add extraneous stories, music, detailed explanations, and elaborate visuals to lessons when our brains are designed for best learning when less loaded.

Why Training Is Too Flabby

I believe that a lot of over inflated training comes from good intentions on the part of instructors including the pressure to "cover the content" in unrealistic time frames, an instructor-centered versus a learner-centered perspective, the urge to make the lessons more engaging by adding interesting stories, and a love affair with the latest training fads and technologies.

As I mentioned in chapter 3, often our clients have unrealistic expectations of what can be achieved in a given time period. In an effort to accommodate, trainers assume the pitcher-of-water role and pour out lots of content for absorption. Unfortunately, our brains don't work that way, and we have learned, sometimes the hard way, that material covered is not material learned. Another problem that trainers often face is a stack of dry content—things like company policy on business transactions, compliance regulations, or procedural training on how to use the order-entry system. To add some sparks of interest, trainers often look to engaging stories and visuals to spice up these courses. Common wisdom suggests that the new generation raised in an age of intensive multimedia and video games has a greater predilection for pizzazz than was the case in the past. The desire to enliven training is fueled by evolving media functionality that makes animations and other effects quite easy. In the end, however, these well-intended additions can have a negative effect on learning.

What Do You Think?

Imagine that you are developing a multimedia lesson on how lightning forms. You prepare several visuals and write some text that describes the process. As you view your draft lesson, you feel it is pretty dull and you want to spice it up. You do a little research on lightning and discover a number of interesting factoids. For example, you are surprised to find that lightning is the leading weather-related cause of death and injury in the United States. In fact, in anyone's lifetime, there is a 1 in 3,000 chance of being struck by lightning. Lightning can even strike an individual when the center of a storm is 10 miles away with blue skies overhead. Armed with these interesting anecdotes about lightning, you enliven your lesson by sprinkling them throughout. What is the impact of anecdotes like these on student interest and on learning? Select the options you think are true:

- ☐ A. The enhanced lesson will lead to better learning because it is more engaging and motivating.
- ☐ B. Learners will find the enhanced lesson more interesting than the basic lesson.
- ☐ C. The basic lesson will lead to better learning because it is lean and stays on target.
- ☐ D. Learning will be the same because both lessons include the critical core content.

The first draft of the lightning lesson consists of a series of still visuals explained by text. Since the lesson is on a process—how lightning works—the instructor decides that an animation explained by audio would be a better way to illustrate what happens. What do you think?

- ☐ A. The animation will result in better learning because it more naturally illustrates change.
- ☐ B. A series of still visuals will result in better learning because the learner can study them at their own pace.
- ☐ C. Learning will be the same in either version become both lessons include the same content.

What Is Too Much?

There are several ways lessons become bloated. Instructors commonly add stories, anecdotes, or themes to spice up a dull presentation. Music is another common addition, especially in multimedia lessons but also in some classrooms. Many individuals prefer to study or work in the presence of background music. In addition, music can add some emotional color. From space odysseys to horror films, music sets the mood. Along with music come visuals that today can be generated easily as animations, three-dimensional computer-generated worlds, or video. These visuals can be so much more polished and engaging than simple line drawings. Finally, instructors often simply provide too much explanation, too many words, too much detail on a topic. In summary, too much of a good thing can involve stories, words, visuals, and music. All are added with the best intentions but run the risk of depressing learning in a brain where less is usually more.

When Stories Defeat Learning

A story is a narrative sequence of events either true or fictitious. From war stories to jokes to anecdotes, stories are common fodder in most training programs. They are used to attract attention, inspire motivation, illustrate a point, dramatize a lesson, or simply spice up dull technical material. Instructors are often encouraged to add stories as effective learning devices. Because they are concrete and often have an emotional tenor, stories are especially memorable and students like them. How many classes can you recall where you don't really remember much about the content but you do remember some of the stories? The memorability of stories makes them a potent psychological device to be used with care.

Evidence on Stories

Mayer (2009) summarizes six experiments in which he compared learning from a basic lesson on lightning formation similar to the one I show in figure 8.1 with the same lesson plus several interesting stories and visuals about the effects of lightning.

For example, there is a brief description and visual showing what happens to an airplane struck by lightning. Later the lesson shows the uniform of a football player who had been struck by lightning. Several of these brief anecdotes were sprinkled throughout the basic lesson to create a more interesting experience. What effect did these spiced up versions have on learning?

Learners rated the lessons with factoids as more interesting than the plain Jane versions. Increased interest, however, did not translate into learning.

Figure 8.1. One Frame from a Lesson on How Lightning Forms Using Line Diagrams and Onscreen Text

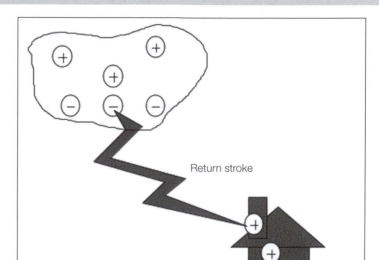

5. Positively charged particles from the ground rush upward along the same path.

From Mayer & Moreno, 1998.

In five of six experiments, learning was dramatically depressed by the addition of interesting facts and visuals about lightning. The median effect size was a very high value of 1.66, signaling considerable damage inflicted by the more interesting lessons. But here is what is important about the stories. Although all of the additions were about lightning, they were not relevant to the instructional goal of building an understanding of how lightning forms.

Stories and the Brain

We don't know for sure why anecdotes like these have a damaging effect on the brain's learning process. It likely stems from the distractions and subsequent disruptions these stories impose. Imagine that you are reading about how clouds first form and then develop ice crystals. Suddenly you are viewing some information about airplanes and lightning. Next you continue to see how negatively charged particles form and fall to the bottom of the cloud. Just as you are connecting the dots, you are seeing and reading about someone struck by lightning. Well, you get the idea. Just as you start to put two and two together, your processing is interrupted by a distracting item that seduces your attention away from the core content. Over time, the cumulative effects of these interruptions corrode learning. Mayer calls the depression of learning resulting from topic-related but goal-irrelevant details a *coherence effect,* as in the disruption of coherence. The evidence and psychology of adding interesting anecdotes unrelated to the learning objective are the basis for my first recommendation.

◆ ◆ ◆

Too Much Guideline 1:

 Avoid adding factoids, visuals, and anecdotes that may be related to the topic but are irrelevant to the learning goal.

◆ ◆ ◆

When Do Stories Help?

I believe that there are situations in which stories have beneficial effects. Unfortunately we lack research evidence to answer questions such as: What kinds of stories are most effective? Are some stories more appropriate for some kinds of learning goals? Does the number and placement of anecdotes in a lesson make a difference? For example, does a dramatic story about an injury or death told at the start of a safety lesson increase attention, learning, and transfer of safety practices? We need a lot more guidance on these issues. For now, I suggest that you keep stories that are relevant to your learning goal, discard stories that are tangential, and avoid placing any dramatic stories in the middle of an explanation where they might disrupt the mental processing needed for understanding.

Do You Listen to Music While Studying?

Are you a person who likes to have music playing in the background while you are working or studying? The benefits of music, especially classical music, have been promoted in popular press articles. What evidence do we have on the effects of music on learning?

Evidence on Music and Learning

Mayer (2009) reports two experimental lessons: one involving lightning formation and one on how brakes work. The basic versions presented the content using narration and animations. The enhanced versions added sounds—both music and environmental sounds appropriate to the lesson topic. The sounds and music were background only and did not obscure the narration. Did music enhance or depress learning? As you can see in figure 8.2, the auditory additions depressed learning.

Figure 8.2. The Average Gain Was 105% in Lessons in Which Extraneous Sounds and Music Were Omitted

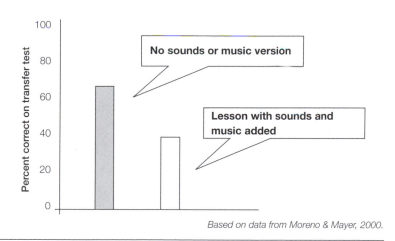

Based on data from Moreno & Mayer, 2000.

Remember that working memory is limited in capacity and has a center for visual and auditory information. When a complex visual is explained by audio narration *plus* sounds and music, the audio center is overloaded and capacity for learning is depressed. The evidence and psychology of learning are the basis for my next recommendation.

◆ ◆ ◆

Too Much Guideline 2:

Think twice about adding extra audio in the form of music when the goal is to help learners build understanding.

◆ ◆ ◆

When I present these experiments at conferences and in workshops, many individuals who routinely listen to music while learning or working get quite irate as this data flies in the face of their own practice. Some claim that music serves as white noise and actually helps them concentrate. They could be right. I am only aware of the two experiments I discussed here that showed negative effects of music on learning. It could be that for some individuals music does help learning. Perhaps we will get additional evidence regarding when or for whom music might be helpful?

Do You Work Too Hard?

One Friday after an intense week of training I was really tired. On reflection I decided that I had actually been working *too hard!* After all, I knew the content. I realized that the workshop participants needed to be doing much more of the work. I had been assuming the water-pitcher role in training figuring that if I gave many detailed explanations presented with a lot of energy and accompanied by many slides, learning would naturally occur. From then on, I started to reverse the workload. I went from two-thirds instructor work–one-third student work to just the opposite. I cut back a lot on explanations. I presented the bare bones and followed up with an exercise. When and where there was confusion on the exercise, I responded with more explanations and examples. When students experienced problems or challenges in the exercises, they were more open to receive additional explanations.

When I tried problem-based learning workshops, I started the session with a short scenario assignment. Teams were given a topic they needed to convert into a multimedia mini lesson. Later, after reviewing course content, teams returned to their case lessons and revised as needed. Having a product assignment from the beginning of the event gave the learners a concrete context to attach the content presented throughout the workshop.

Evidence About Explanations

Using the lightning content, Mayer tested the learning effects of a very concise lesson with a version containing a much more detailed explanation. Take a look at figures 8.1 and 8.3 to compare the lean and inflated versions.

As you can see, the lean version in figure 8.1 consisted of a simple visual with just a few words as a caption. In total, the lean version contained about 80 words. In contrast, the detailed version added more than 500

Figure 8.3. One Frame from an Expanded Lesson on How Lightning Forms with Additional Explanatory Text

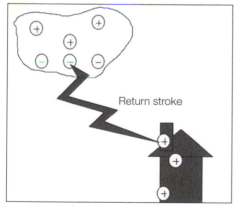

Return stroke

As the stepped leader nears the ground, it induces an opposite charge so positively charged particles from the ground rush upward along the same path. This upward motion of the current is the return stroke and it reaches the cloud in about 70 micro-seconds. The return stroke produces the bright light that people notice in a flash of lightning, but the current moves so quickly that its upward motion cannot be perceived. The lightning flash usually consists of an electrical potential of hundreds of millions of volts. The air along the lightning channel is heated briefly to a very high temperature. Such intense heating causes the air to expand explosively, producing a sound wave we call thunder.

5. Positively charged particles from the ground rush upward along the same path.

From Mayer, Bove et al., 1996.

words to the captioned figures. In three experiments learning was better from the more concise versions with effect sizes ranging from .70 to .98.

There are a couple of reasons the brain is better off with leaner explanations. First, the limits of working memory suggest that you provide only the amount of information needed to communicate the core content leaving capacity for processing that content. When providing lean explanations, memory space would be available to read the words, look at the visual, integrate the meaning of the words and visual, and connect that meaning to the unfolding process. In other words there would be capacity to connect the dots. Second, more words may leave the learner more passive. Reading a detailed and very full explanation may actually discourage a high level of processing compared to a bare bones approach. Based on the evidence and the psychology of explanations I suggest the following guideline.

◆ ◆ ◆

Too Much Guideline 3:

Keep explanations concise; use just enough words to present content. Use the time gained to assign activities which can lead to a "moment of need" on the part of learners.

◆ ◆ ◆

When Visuals Overload the Brain

From photographs to 3-D drawings, from video to animations, modern technology makes production of elaborate visuals quite easy. And the ubiquitous high end visuals in popular media might encourage us to incorporate them into training environments. What is the value added of complex visuals?

Simple Versus Complex Static Visuals

Imagine that you want to build an accurate understanding of how the heart circulates blood. You begin with a pretest that asks learners to sketch a diagram and write an explanation of blood circulation. You find a mix of ideas—many inaccurate or incomplete—and categorize them. For example, some of the drawings show no understanding other than that blood does come out of the heart. Others capture the idea that blood not only comes out of the heart, but it also returns, but how it does so is sketchy. You then prepare three versions of a lesson on how blood circulates. One is a text explanation. The other two versions add visuals similar to those shown in figure 8.4.

Figure 8.4. Two Graphics from Lessons on How Blood Circulates through the Heart

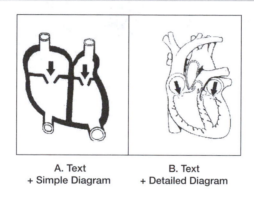

A. Text
+ Simple Diagram

B. Text
+ Detailed Diagram

From Butcher, 2006

As you can see, one visual is a simple line drawing and the other visual is a more realistic 3-D drawing. Learners are randomly assigned to one of the three versions. After they complete the lesson, they are asked to explain and sketch blood circulation. You can compare the changes in their understanding from the pretest to the posttest. Which lesson version resulted in best improvement of mental models? What do you think?

- ☐ The text version because it included the most concise content.
- ☐ The text plus line drawing version because it included a simple diagram.
- ☐ The text plus 3-D drawing version because it had the most technically accurate depiction of blood flow.

I summarize the results from this experiment in figure 8.5.

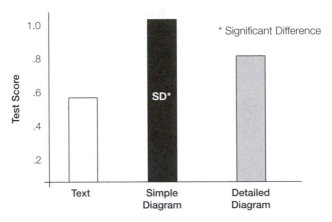

Figure 8.5. Accuracy in Circulation Mental Models After Viewing Three Lesson Versions

Based on data from Butcher, 2006.

We learned in chapter 5 that relevant visuals enhance learning through dual messages to the brain—one through words and one through pictures. Therefore, both lesson versions with visuals of the heart resulted in better learning than the text-only version. However, the simple line drawing was more effective than the more detailed 3-D depiction. When learning how something works, the details in the realistic drawing did not augment understanding and in fact may have led to confusion.

Static Visuals Versus Animations

We saw in the heart circulation experiment that a simpler visual resulted in better learning than a more complex visual. Let's look at how static visuals and animations affect learning. Imagine that you want to teach how a toilet works—a potentially very useful piece of knowledge. You could show a series of static visuals explained by text or you could play an animation with audio narration. At first glance, the animated version would seem like a more effective approach as it can readily show the movement at the various flushing stages. But this is not what the experiments revealed. In four different lessons involving explanations of toilet flushing, lightning formation, how brakes work, and wave formation, the static versions led to learning that *was better than or as good as* the animated versions (Mayer, Hegarty et al. 2005).

It's not hard to see that an animation conveys a great deal of complex visual information that in the experiments above ran continuously. In contrast, the static graphics were simpler, and learners could view them at their own pace. The animation provided a flood of information that quickly over loaded memory capacity.

In addition to the sheer amount of information, it is also possible that learners are more actively engaged in the stills than in the animations. Often when we view an animation, we go into "couch potato" mode, conditioned no doubt by years of watching television in a passive mindset. In contrast, as we view a series of static visuals to understand the process, our brains get involved in connecting each stage with the ones to follow. Ironically, what we would commonly classify as an old-fashioned medium—for example, still pictures on paper—might engage the brain more than a modern treatment with animation.

Before you trash all of your animation ideas, keep in mind a couple of adjustments that can make animations less intense. First, include controls for pauses or even automatically pause the animation periodically allowing the learner to replay or continue the display themselves. Letting the learner manage the pace of the animation might attenuate the potential adverse effects of visual overload. Second, use various visual cues such as circles or color to draw attention to the relevant part of the animation that is under discussion.

Based on evidence we have to date on the use of animations to explain how things work, I offer the following suggestion.

◆ ◆ ◆

Too Much Guideline 4:

When your goal is to build an understanding of how something works, use simpler visuals that allow learner control over pacing.

◆ ◆ ◆

Animations for Illustrating Procedures

Also consider your instructional goal. In all of the experiments summarized above, the goal was to build understanding of how something works. Understanding requires a deep level of processing to build a mental model. However, what if you are teaching someone how to perform a procedure such as tying knots, assembling equipment, or working with new software? Might animations be more effective for this type of goal? Ayers et al. (2009) compared learning of motor skills such as tying a knot, or solving a 3-D puzzle problem from a series of stills versus an animated demonstration. No practice was given. Learners viewed the demonstrations and then were tested without reference to the visuals. For both motor tasks, learning was about twice as good from the animated demonstrations. Researchers are postulating that working memory has another processing center in addition to the visual and phonetic centers I discussed in chapter 2. It is called a *mirror-neuron system*, and it is dedicated exclusively to human movement. That is the reason that an animation of a motor skill to teach a procedure might not overload working memory whereas an animation of a process to illustrate a process will.

We need more research on the use of animations to teach procedures. However, based on what we know so far, I offer the following suggestion.

◆ ◆ ◆

Too Much Guideline 5:

When your goal is to teach a procedure, use dynamic visuals that offer controls such as pause and replay.

◆ ◆ ◆

The Bottom Line

We started our discussion with two comparisons of treatments for a lesson on lightning formation. In one treatment we discussed the effects of a "just the facts" lesson compared to a lesson that spiced up the content with interesting anecdotes sprinkled throughout. Here are my comments:

☐ A. The enhanced lesson will lead to better learning because it is more engaging and motivational.
FALSE. Although learners do find these lessons more interesting, the distracting effects of anecdotes have been shown to depress learning.

☐ B. Learners will find the enhanced lesson more interesting than the basic lesson.
TRUE. However, increased interest does not necessarily translate into better learning.

☐ C. The basic lesson will lead to better learning because it is lean and stays on target.
TRUE. When understanding is the goal, better results come from lessons that stay on message.

☐ D. Learning will be the same because both lessons include the critical core content.
FALSE. We see throughout this book that how content is presented makes a huge difference to learning. A worthwhile goal is to find anecdotes and visuals that both add interest and *promote learning.*

The second question compared learning from a series of still visuals to animations. Here are my comments:

☐ A. The animation will result in better learning because it more naturally illustrates change.
FALSE. Although this conclusion seems intuitive, uncontrolled animations can overload memory and thereby depress understanding.

☐ B. A series of still visuals will result in better learning because the learner can study them at their own pace.
TRUE. Based on evidence to date, learning is better from a series of stills than from an animated explanation of a process.

☐ C. Learning will be the same in either version become both lessons include the same content.
FALSE. See my comment to the previous option D.

Applying Less Is More to Your Training

We've seen that when it comes to explanations, visuals, stories, and music, in many cases learning is better when you offer learners a leaner lesson with concise explanations and simple but relevant visuals. At the same time, avoid anecdotes that don't directly contribute to the learning goal as well as extraneous audio in the form of background music.

Use the following checklist as you start to plan your lessons and when reviewing a draft lesson.

Does my lesson or presentation . . .

☐ focus on a few topics that can be taught in a relatively short time frame?

☐ maintain concise explanation?

☐ use simpler visuals to illustrate how things work?

☐ use dynamic visuals to demonstrate procedures?

☐ include controls with all dynamic visuals?

☐ avoid anecdotes that are not relevant to the lesson goal?

☐ avoid background music during episodes that require mental concentration?

For More Information

Clark, R.C. (2008). *Building Expertise,* 3d ed. San Francisco: Pfeiffer. See ch. 6.

Clark, R.C., & R.E. Mayer (2008b). *e-Learning & the Science of Instruction,* 2d ed. San Francisco: Pfeiffer. See ch. 7.

Mayer, R.E. (2009). *Multimedia Learning,* 2d ed. New York: Cambridge University Press. See ch. 4.

Part III

Evidence-Based Use of Examples and Practice

In chapters 9 and 10 I focus on proven guidelines to maximize the benefits from two of the most potent instructional methods: examples and practice.

◆ ◆ ◆

Accelerate Expertise with Examples

◆ ◆ ◆

Chapter 9

Accelerate Expertise with Examples

actose is a complex sugar found in milk. To digest lactose, you need lactase, an enzyme that breaks lactose into two sugar molecules: glucose and galactose. Individuals lacking this enzyme have lactose intolerance. Unable to digest milk, they suffer from various gastrointestinal symptoms. Lactase is but one of about 4,000 different enzymes that serve as catalysts of essential physiological processes. Catalysts speed up the rate of chemical reactions but are themselves unaffected. Examples are learning catalysts.

by Ann Kwinn & C. Kwinn

You might be able to learn without them. However, adding examples to lessons has been proven to dramatically accelerate learning!

In this chapter we will unlock the secrets of exploiting examples for different types of content and different learners. We will see how you can use examples not only to improve learning outcomes but also to decrease instructional time.

The Power of Examples

Whether your goal is to provide information or to help staff acquire new skills, *examples* are useful. But in training designed to build skills, examples are not only useful—they are essential! Right now you might be thinking that you do use examples. After all, examples are a commonly used training method. However, are you fully exploiting the hidden power of examples to accelerate learning? Few trainers know of recent research on how to fully leverage examples. By applying the techniques I describe in this chapter, you can extend the potential of your examples by considering the what, when, where, and for whom of examples.

What Do You Think?

Which lesson plan in figure 9.1 do you think would be more effective?

Figure 9.1. Two Lesson Versions that Differ Regarding Examples

Lesson Version A	Lesson Version B
Explanation	Explanation
Example 1	Example
Practice 1	Practice 1
Example 2	Practice 2
Practice 2	Practice 3
Example 3	Practice 4
Practice 3	Practice 5

As you can see, in both lessons you get an equal number of problems to review (six in each lesson). But in lesson version A, half the problems are in the form of examples and half in the form of practice, whereas in lesson version B you get a lot more practice! Which lesson will take longer to complete? Which lesson will lead to better learning?

John Sweller, one of our most influential contemporary instructional researchers, studied the effects of examples on learning. He took a traditional algebra lesson containing one or two examples followed by many problem assignments and converted several of the practice exercises into a step-by-step example like the one in figure 9.2. Instructional psychologists call demonstrations like the one in figure 9.2 *worked examples*. A worked example is simply a demonstration that illustrates the steps the learner must take to complete a task or solve a problem. In addition to showing each stage in the problem solution, most worked examples also include an explanation either in text or audio depending on the delivery medium. For the worked example shown in figure 9.2, the instructor might begin by saying, "First, we move all numbers to the right side of the equation."

Figure 9.2. A Worked Example of an Algebra Problem

$$5X + 3 = 6X$$
1. $5X = 6X - 3$
2. $-X = -3$
3. $X = 3$

Sweller and Cooper (1985) compared learning from traditional lessons containing mostly practice to their example–practice pairs lesson version. You won't be surprised to learn that the traditional lesson with lots of practice took longer to complete. In fact the versions that incorporated more practice took six times longer than the versions that alternated examples and practice. But did that time and effort invested in solving practice problems pay off in better learning? Surprisingly, they found that learners studying the all-practice lesson *made twice as many errors* on a test than learners studying the example–practice pairs version! A combination of examples and practice led to faster and better learning than working lots of practice problems.

By replacing some practice exercises with worked out examples, you can accelerate learning. That's why I call worked examples learning catalysts. The many experiments that have shown the benefits of worked out examples support my first recommendation.

◆ ◆ ◆

Examples Guideline 1:

Save time and improve learning by replacing some practice exercises with worked out examples.

◆ ◆ ◆

Examples and the Brain

How do examples work? In chapter 2 we learned that our working memory (our brain's active processor) has a very limited capacity. Do you recall working all those homework problems in your math class? Solving lots of problems is hard work! When working memory capacity is tied up working lots of problems, there is little resource left over for learning. However, imagine that instead of working a problem, you are reviewing an example. Your working memory is not bogged down trying to solve the problem. Instead it is free to carefully study the example and learn from it. In fact, by providing an example as a model, the student has a perfect opportunity to learn from it. Then by following the example with a similar practice assignment, the student can confirm that they have learned correctly!

Examples for Routine Tasks

In chapter 3 I discussed two types of skills: routine tasks also known as *procedures* and *strategic tasks* that require judgment and problem solving.

For routine tasks, your examples should mirror the work environment as closely as possible. This means incorporating the equipment, application screens, forms that would be used on the job into your example.

How should you format your words and visuals in examples for best learning? As I mentioned in chapter 6, learning is best when you use audio narration to explain examples that involve graphics. As we discussed in chapter 8, we have evidence that animations are *not* the best method to build new knowledge about how things work. In contrast, we are accumulating evidence that animations may be the best route to teach procedural skills that involve motion.

Animations Versus Still Graphics for Routine Task Demonstrations

When using dynamic visuals to illustrate a procedure, be sure to allow the learners control over play of the demonstration. Provide controls to pause, replay, reverse, or change speed of the demonstrations as needed. Schwan and Riempp (2004) found that learning to tie nautical knots from video examples was *much* faster when the video demonstrations included controls. In their experiment learners watched a video of how to tie knots for as long as they wished and could practice tying the knot after the video was stopped. After completing the learning phase, each participant demonstrated how to tie the knot. Everyone learned how to tie all of the knots. However, those who viewed the videos *without controls* took from 66 to 95 percent longer to learn the skills! My next guideline is based on the research on examples for procedures.

◆ ◆ ◆

Examples Guideline 2:

For routine tasks, create demonstrations that incorporate the context of the workplace. Describe graphics with audio (narration or instructor) and use dynamic visuals (video or animation) with controls to demonstrate steps.

◆ ◆ ◆

Examples for Strategic Tasks

Read the tumor story shown in the following box and list some possible solutions.

The Tumor Problem

Suppose you are a doctor faced with a patient who has a malignant tumor in his stomach. It is impossible to operate on the patient, but, unless the tumor is destroyed, the patient will die. There is a kind of ray that at a sufficiently high intensity can destroy the tumor. Unfortunately, at this intensity, the healthy tissue that the rays pass through on the way to the tumor will also be destroyed. At lower intensities, the rays are harmless to healthy tissue but will not affect the tumor either. How can the rays be used to destroy the tumor without injuring the healthy tissue?

Source: Gick and Holyoak (1980).

In a classic experiment, Gick and Holyoak (1980) asked a number of people to solve the tumor problem. Before reviewing it, the experimental subjects read several other stories. One of these stories told of a general who wanted to invade a fortress. Because the roads to the fortress were mined, he had to split his troops into small groups, each attacking from a different path and thus not triggering the mines. What is the commonality between the tumor and fortress stories? They are both solved by a common principle: convergence. The tumor problem is resolved by aiming several low intensity rays to converge at the site of the tumor but not harm the intermediate tissues.

Do you think that the individuals who read the fortress story were able to apply the convergence principle to solve the tumor problem? It turned out that very few were successful—only about 30 percent. The context of the fortress story is so different from the tumor story that most individuals fail to see the connection. Imagine now that the fortress story represents your training event. You have presented an example to illustrate a convergence principle. Further imagine that the tumor problem represents a situation the learner faces on the job. With training that only uses one type of problem, transfer to a job situation with different surface features will be quite limited.

When teaching strategic skills such as making a sale, diagnosing a problem, or writing a report, each job situation will be a bit different. Unlike routine tasks where the work setting will remain fairly consistent, the context will vary in strategic tasks. For the salesperson, the customer, the product mix, the setting will vary a bit with each encounter. How can we best ensure that workers will have sufficient flexibility to tackle these ever-changing situations?

We can get a clue from Gick and Holyoak who boosted the number of individuals who could solve the tumor problem. Here's how they did it. They provided readers not only with the fortress story but also with a fire fighter story that required multiple hoses aiming into the fire to extinguish the blaze. After reviewing the two stories, participants were asked to draw a picture or write a couple of sentences that represented the common element (convergence) in both stories. After this "training" exercise, many more of the readers were able to solve the tumor problem! The secret is to provide several examples that illustrate the underlying principles but at the same time vary their cover stories.

This technique is called *varied context* examples. As the brain processes several examples and is required to articulate the commonalities, long-term memory abstracts a sufficiently flexible understanding of the principles to apply to other relevant situations. For best results from examples for strategic tasks, apply my third principle.

◆ ◆ ◆

Examples Guideline 3:

For strategic tasks provide several examples that illustrate the guidelines of the task but vary the storyline. Assign an activity to encourage abstraction of the common underlying principles.

◆ ◆ ◆

Consider Animations for Examples That Involve Interpersonal Skills

What is the best way to format your examples? We have some growing evidence that examples for tasks that involve complex social skills such as supervision, sales, or teaching may benefit from animated displays.

Moreno and Ortegano-Layne (2008) developed a lesson for student teachers on principles to help their students process new information effectively. To help student teachers apply the principles, the research team developed several examples that illustrated teachers applying the guidelines in the classroom. Participants in the control group received no examples. The examples were presented in one of three formats: text, video, or computer animation. The student teachers then responded to an application test asking them to describe how they could make their own instruction more effective by applying the principles taught. Which example format do you think led to best learning?

☐ A. The text example was best because learners could review it at their own pace.

☐ B. The video example was best because it was the most realistic.

☐ C. The computer animation example was best because it was a simpler visual than the video example.

As you can see in figure 9.3, all of the student teachers who received an example learned more than those who did not. However, the visual

Figure 9.3. Learning from Teaching Examples in Diverse Formats

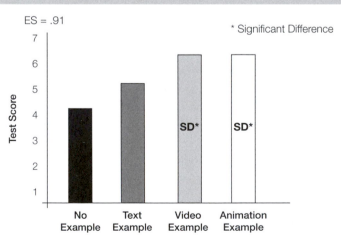

Based on data from Moreno & Ortegano-Layne, 2008.

examples—both video and computer animated—resulted in better learning than the text examples. Based on our limited evidence, either B or C could be correct. The research team, in fact, favored the animated version because it omitted extraneous visual "noise" that appeared in the video. Participants in this experiment also rated the quality of their lesson versions. Ratings showed that learners liked the visual examples—both video and animation better than text examples.

We need more research on the best modes to use for routine and strategic task examples. However, based on what we know so far, I recommend that tasks that involve complex interpersonal skills such as customer service, sales, management, and teaching be illustrated with animated examples (computer animations or video).

When Examples Can Harm Learning

We've seen in prior chapters that some instructional techniques such as graphics are powerful aids for novices but aren't much help for learners with more background knowledge. Which of the following statements do you think is most accurate regarding who benefits the most from examples? Check all that apply.

- ☐ A. Novices benefit from examples more than experts.
- ☐ B. Novices and experts benefit equally from examples.
- ☐ C. Experts benefit from examples more than novices.
- ☐ D. Experts are better off without examples.

Kalyuga and his colleagues (2001) measured learning from training on how to write programs for relay circuits. The learners who were beginners were divided into two groups: an example-problem group (similar to lesson version A in figure 9.1) and an all problem group (similar to lesson version B in figure 9.1). Learning was measured at several times as the group gained expertise.

During the beginning stages, learners benefited greatly from studying examples. A funny thing happened over time though. As they became more experienced, not only did the examples *not* help, they actually depressed learning! Based on this evidence, the correct answers above are A and D.

Instructional psychologists call this an *expertise reversal effect*. Expertise reversal means that some methods useful for novices not only don't help those with more experience, but they actually hurt their learning! The evidence we have accumulated on expertise reversal leads to the next principle.

◆ ◆ ◆

Examples Guideline 4:

Use worked examples for novice learners. For learners with experience in the content, emphasize practice assignments more than examples.

◆ ◆ ◆

More About Examples and the Brain

Compared to working lots of problems, examples benefit learners because working memory is free to study the example and learn from it. The example serves as a learning catalyst by providing a substitute for the missing knowledge of the novice learner. But a more experienced learner already has some relevant understanding. They are better off applying their own process to a practice assignment than reviewing a demonstration that at best just duplicates and at worst might actually interfere with their own unique approach to the task.

Use Faded Worked Examples to Accommodate Growing Expertise

A useful technique you can use to accommodate learners who are building expertise is called *fading*. Here's how it works. Imagine an example with four steps. You begin by providing a completely worked out example for the learner to study. You follow with a second example in which the first steps have been worked out and the learner needs to finish it. With each new example the learner completes more of it until they are doing a full problem assignment. Figure 9.4 models a faded worked example for a three-step task. Remember that since strategic tasks benefit from varied context, each of your examples in the faded series should use different scenarios.

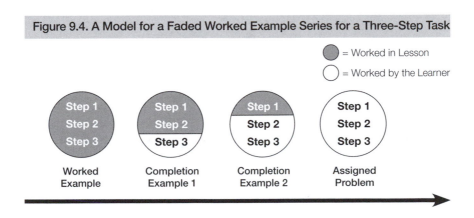

Figure 9.4. A Model for a Faded Worked Example Series for a Three-Step Task

Research experiments reported by Atkinson and his colleagues (2003) showed that learning was better from lessons using faded worked examples than from lessons that provided example–problem pairs.

How to Make Examples Engaging

We've seen that examples are one of your most powerful instructional allies. But there is one problem. Many learners either skip examples completely or don't process them very deeply. Chi (2000) showed that higher scoring physics students studied examples carefully, investing the effort to explain the examples to themselves. In contrast, poorer students tended to ignore examples or just restate what the example said. You can boost the instructional potential of your examples by encouraging your learners to study them carefully. How? By inserting or asking questions next to the worked out steps, you motivate learners to review the steps in order to answer the question. Figure 9.5 illustrates a question added to a geometry worked example.

Atkinson and his colleagues (2003) found that including the questions with the worked examples improved learning.

Figure 9.5. Adding a Question Encourages Meaningful Processing of an Example

EXAMPLE:

Find the area of a circle when the diameter is 8

Step 1. Formula: $A = \pi R^2$

Step 2. Radius = 8/2 = 4

Step 3. A = 3.12 times 16

Step 4. A = 49.92

QUESTION:

In step 2, why was 8 divided by 2?

A. Because the radius must be squared

B. Because the radius is half the diameter

C. Because pi equals 4

D. Because 4 is the square root of 16

There are many forms of questions that could help your learners squeeze more value out of your examples. Try questions that stimulate reflection on the principles or rules behind your example. My final principle in this chapter recommends you energize your examples with associated questions.

◆ ◆ ◆

Examples Guideline 4:

Add questions to steps in your worked out examples to encourage learners to process them deeply.

◆ ◆ ◆

The Bottom Line

We began the chapter comparing two lesson plans shown in figure 9.1. Version A followed an explanation with a series of example–problem pairs. Version B followed an explanation with one example and lots of practice problems. Which is better?

Based on quite a bit of evidence, lesson version A is better. *However, version A is only better for novice learners who will benefit from demonstrations.* More experienced learners would be better off with lesson version B.

Applying Examples to Your Training

We've seen evidence that replacing some practice problems with worked out examples both speeds up and improves learning. We've also seen some techniques to get more mileage out of your examples. Use this checklist to guide the examples you prepare for your training:

Examples for Routine or Strategic Tasks

☐ For *routine tasks*, provide demonstrations that accurately reflect the tools and techniques of the job.

☐ For *routine tasks involving movement*, use animation.

☐ *Allow control of the animated display* such as stopping, replaying, and slow motion.

☐ For *strategic tasks*, provide worked examples that vary the context.

☐ For *strategic tasks that involve interpersonal skills*, use computer animations or video to present worked examples.

Examples for Different Learners

☐ Provide worked examples for novice learners.

☐ For experienced learners, assign practice in lieu of examples.

☐ Use a series of examples that assign increasing numbers of steps to the learner (faded worked examples) to accommodate the growth of expertise.

For All Examples

☐ Encourage engagement in your examples by asking questions that require the learner to process the example in a manner consistent with your learning goals.

For More Information

Clark, R.C. & R.E. Mayer (2008b). *e-Learning & the Science of Instruction*, 2d ed. San Francisco: Pfeiffer. See ch. 10.

Clark, R.C. (2008). *Building Expertise*. 3d ed. San Francisco: Pfeiffer. See chs. 6 and 9.

♦ ♦ ♦

Maximize the Benefits of Practice

The Power of Practice

What Is Practice?

What Is Effective Practice?

Practice and the Brain

How Much Practice?

When to Assign Practice

How to Group Practice Problems

Feedback

The Bottom Line

Applying Practice to your Training

♦ ♦ ♦

Chapter 10

Maximize the Benefits of Practice

"One way of looking at this might be that, for 42 years, I've been making small regular deposits in this bank of experience: education and training. And on January 15, the balance was sufficient so that I could make a very large withdrawal."

—Capt. Chesley "Sully"
Sullenberger
Pilot of US Airways Flight 1549,
CBS News, February 10, 2009

The mind needs time to practice in order to learn.

No, I'm not ready yet! I'm still trying to process the last load!

by Ann Kwinn & C. Kwinn

From music to chess to golf, evidence from world-class performers reinforces the saying that expertise is "99 percent perspiration and 1 percent inspiration," to borrow a phrase from Thomas Edison.

In this chapter we will look at evidence behind five core guidelines to help you maximize the benefits of practice during training. Specifically we will review 1) what kind of practice works best, 2) how much practice to include in your lessons, 3) where to place practice, 4) how to group practice, and 5) the role of feedback to practice responses.

The Power of Practice

From Captain Sullenberger to Tiger Woods, world-class performers did not achieve their proficiency haphazardly. Star performers start young. Tiger Woods was golfing as a toddler, and Captain Sully had his first pilot license at the age of 16. Second, they invest countless hours in regular focused practice even after reaching high performance levels. In fact, research on the best musicians, athletes, and chess players consistently finds they require a minimum of 10 years of sustained and focused practice to reach their peak performance period (Ericcson 2006)

Naturally aptitude and attributes play a role. I'm a basketball fan. But at 5'2" (not to mention my age!), I doubt that any amount of practice will make me even a mediocre performer. Tiger Woods' 6'2" lean frame gives him the height and flexibility to leverage his swing. Captain Sully is a smart man having qualified for Mensa when he was 12. Aptitude not withstanding, for the most part we underestimate the role of practice in building competence and in fact rarely reach the full potential of our natural gifts. It's true. Expertise is 99 percent perspiration and 1 percent inspiration!

What Do You Think?

Place a check next to each statement you believe is true about practice:

☐ A. The more the practice, the better the learning.

☐ B. Six practice exercises placed at the end of the lesson will lead to better learning than the same six exercises distributed throughout the lesson.

☐ C. When teaching two topics, it's better to group practice questions according to topic than to mix questions for both topics in the same section.

☐ D. "List the five steps to construct a formula in Excel" is an effective practice exercise.

☐ E. Learners benefit from knowing whether their answers are correct or incorrect after responding to a practice question.

What Is Practice?

Practice is an overt response to assignments intended to build goal-relevant knowledge and/or skills. Responding to a multiple choice exercise, repeating 20 free throws in basketball, engaging in role play, working collaboratively on a case study, or completing an online drag-and-drop activity are but a few examples of the diversity of practice formats. Let's look at this definition in more detail.

First, to qualify as practice, the learner must make some kind of response. For the purposes of formal training, that response usually produces a visible product—one that can be evaluated for accuracy. Naturally learners can also practice silently such as repeating a vocabulary word when learning a foreign language. However, to maximize the benefits of feedback, I recommend an overt response.

Second, practice is a specific assignment intended to help learners bridge performance gaps. Here I distinguish between practice in general and "deliberate" practice that focuses on specific skill gaps. We all know the classic recreational golfer. She accumulates many practice hours over time but never improves beyond a baseline that typically falls far short of her capabilities. Deliberate practice requires an analysis of skill gaps and an intense focus on those gaps, usually with the help of a skilled coach or instructor (Ericcson 2006).

What Is Effective Practice?

There are two types of practice: 1) recall assignments that ask the learner to repeat the content of the lesson, and 2) application assignments that ask the learner to apply knowledge or perform job tasks. I label recall assignments "regurgitate" exercises because they ask the learner to spit back what they were told in the lesson. In contrast, application assignments prompt the learner to respond in a manner similar to the requirements of the job.

Figure 10.1. Excel Formula Practice: Versions A, B, and C

Practice Version A

List the 3 features of an Excel formula.

Practice Version B

Select the correctly formatted Excel formula:

= 4C x 9F

= 4C/3D

2B + 3A =

Practice Version C

Enter the formula in the spreadsheet to calculate 3rd quarter profit

For example, in figure 10.1, compare three practice assignments from an Excel training session. Which exercises do you think are most effective?

The practice version A is a recall assignment. It promotes rote learning. Recalling the features of an Excel formula does not mean that the learner can identify or construct a viable formula. Version B is a closer reflection of actual job performance because it asks the learner to identify a correctly formatted formula. This is a useful exercise for an important knowledge topic associated with using Excel. However, you would not want to rely on this practice alone because it fails to require learners to actually perform the task of constructing and entering a formula. Practice version C comes the closest to the requirements of the job.

Why not assign all three types of practice? After all doesn't one need to know (that is, memorize) the formula features to be able to construct a formula? With a few exceptions, I discourage regurgitation types of practice exercises such as version A for several reasons. First, rote learning does not lead to understanding, and most workplace performance benefits from understanding. Second, basic facts and procedure steps can often be provided on a working aid to minimize reliance on recall. And, third, most trainers have limited time to achieve training goals. It makes sense to leverage that time by assigning practice that will directly lead to effective job performance.

Practice and the Brain

Recall from chapter 2 the three critical features of working memory: active processor, limited capacity, and dual channels (one for words and one for visuals). To translate new knowledge and skills from the instructional environment into long-term memory, working memory must actively process the content. This active processing is supported by your practice exercises. But it's not enough to get new knowledge and skills encoded into long-term memory. Those knowledge and skills must be retrieved from long-term memory later when needed on the job. Therefore, as you plan practice you need to consider both how to get knowledge and skills into long-term memory and back out again.

Retrieval is the basis for what instructional psychologists call transfer of learning. New knowledge and skills processed at the time of learning must transfer later to job settings. Fortunately for the passengers of US Airways Flight 1549, Captain Sullenberger was able to make a rapid and effective transfer of his years of accumulated knowledge and skills. Tragically, for the passengers in Continental Flight 3407, the pilot had no hands-on training on the control maneuvers needed to correct an impending stall. He may have had some classroom knowledge of the appropriate responses, but this knowledge was not retrieved from memory at the instant it was needed.

Embed Retrieval Hooks During Learning

Memory retrieval hooks must be implanted at the time of learning. It's too late to embed them later. Recall our calendar demonstration from chapter 3. You had no problem recalling the months of the year chronologically because your memory hooks involve a time sequence. For workforce learning, the retrieval hooks are the sights, kinesthetics, and sounds of the workplace. In other words, it's all about context. To optimize transfer of learning, you need to embed the context of the job into your practice exercises. Rather than asking learners to recall the steps to perform a task or list the name of the parts of the equipment, embed the job context into the exercise by asking learners to perform the task or circle the part of the equipment that performs a specific function.

Based on the evidence and the psychology of learning, I offer my first recommendation.

Practice Guideline 1:

Incorporate the context of the job to create practice exercises that require application rather than recall of content.

One good way to implement this guideline is to develop job-realistic scenarios that embed the knowledge and skills of the job. Some scenarios can serve as a context for worked examples. Additional scenarios can be the basis for various practice assignments.

How Much Practice?

Practice takes time and time is money, so deciding how much practice to include is an important issue.

Top performers like world-class athletes maintain a regular and rigorous practice regimen. Does this mean that the more we practice, the better we get? The answer is yes and no. In fact, you do continue to improve over time with practice—but at a diminishing rate. Instructional psychologists call this the *Power Law of Practice*. The power law means that skills build rapidly during the first few practice sessions. However, as practice continues, the rate of skill proficiency slows. The greatest improvements will accrue from the first practice sessions. Afterward, improvement continues but at a slower rate.

Evidence on Amount of Practice and Learning

Rohrer and Taylor (2006) studied learning of a mathematical procedure from two different practice regimens. All participants viewed a tutorial that demonstrated how to solve several example problems. Then half the participants had a practice session consisting of three problems and the other half completed nine practice problems. Some participants from each group were tested right away and the others were tested four weeks later. Figure 10.2 shows the results.

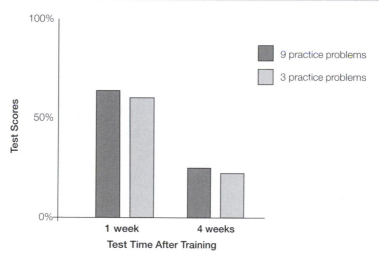

Figure 10.2. Learning Outcomes from Lower and Higher Amount of Practice

Based on data from Rohrer & Taylor, 2006.

Everyone did better on the immediate test than on the delayed test. However, there were no real differences on either the immediate *or* the delayed test between the low and high practice groups. These results are an example of the Power Law of Practice. The research team concludes that "the minimal effect of over-learning on retention can be interpreted as an instance of diminishing returns. That is, with each additional amount of practice devoted to a single concept, there was an ever smaller increase in test performance" (Rohrer and Taylor 2006, 1218).

A Time for Over-Learning

There are situations that benefit from extensive practice that leads to automaticity. Landing an aircraft is one example. Not only are the consequences of error very serious, but also multiple actions must be taken very quickly. There is no time to refer to a working aid to decide what to do next. Over-learning is expensive because it requires sufficient drill and practice to build automaticity. In many workplace settings, automaticity can evolve naturally through repetitive performance on the job—in other words through experience. However, in some situations such as landing an aircraft, the first solo landing must be pretty good. Over-learning is justified.

Over-learning may also be needed when the final task is so complex that the underlying component skills must be automatic to free up working memory resources to devote to it. I feel that the most important skill I learned in high school was typing. At least it is the one skill that I have continued to use more than 40 years later. With automated typing skills, I can devote most of my working memory capacity to expressing my ideas. My typing skill, however, was an expensive investment requiring many hours of daily practice.

You will need to decide whether over-learning through extensive and time-consuming practice is warranted for your learning goals.

So how much practice do you need? There is no universal rule. Based on the evidence and psychology of repetitive practice, consider the following recommendations.

◆ ◆ ◆

Practice Guideline 2:

Adjust the amount of practice in your training based on the following criteria:

A. Consequences of error. If serious, you need more rather than less practice.

B. Acceptability of a job aid. If yes, then fewer practice exercises might be appropriate.

C. Complexity of the work. If high, drill and practice might be needed to automate requisite subskills.

◆ ◆ ◆

When to Assign Practice

Have you ever crammed for an exam? Most of us have at one time or another waited until the last minute and then studied intensively. And in most cases, cramming does work. You do pass the test. On other occasions you may have been more organized and scheduled your study periods for several weeks (or at least days) prior to the exam. Since you pass the test either way, what are the benefits of a more spread out study schedule?

Cramming is an example of what instructional psychologists call *massed practice*. Massed practice simply means all of the practice occurs in one lump—usually at the end of the class session or lesson. The alternative is *spaced practice* in which the same amount of practice is distributed over a longer period of time. For example, rather than working all practice at the end of the lesson, the exercises are distributed throughout. Which plan is best?

Evidence for Massed Versus Spaced Practice

Rohrer and Taylor (2006) compared learning of math skills from 10 practice problems. One group did all 10 problems in a single session. A second group practiced five problems in one week and the other five in the following week. Learners were tested one week after the final practice session and again four weeks after the final practice session. Take a look at figure 10.3 and indicate your conclusions:

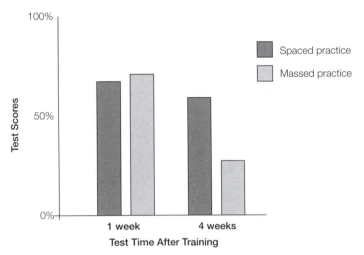

Figure 10.3. Immediate and Delayed Learning from Spaced and Massed Practice

Based on data from Rohrer & Taylor, 2006.

Your interpretation:

☐ A. Spaced practice works better for immediate learning.
☐ B. Spaced practice works better for long-term learning.
☐ C. Massed practice works better for immediate learning.
☐ D. Massed practice works better for long-term learning.

As you can see from the research results, cramming (massed practice) works in the short term but not for longer-term retention. The correct answer to the previous question is option B. Keep in mind that as an instructor, you won't see any benefits to spacing during or right after the training. It's only in the longer term that spaced practice assignments reveal their advantages. As trainers we rarely see how our lessons translate into job performance. Without data such as that shown in figure 10.3, we would never know the advantage of spaced assignments.

Spacing Your Practice Sessions

An easy way to reap the benefits of spaced practice is to simply schedule your exercises differently. For example, imagine you are teaching a two-day course with eight lessons. In lesson 2 of this course you teach the first skill and include 10 practice questions at the end of the lesson. In lesson 3 you teach the next skill and include 10 practice questions to reinforce that lesson. This is a typical practice schedule.

A simple adjustment can take advantage of spaced scheduling. At the end of lesson 2, include only five of the 10 practice questions you created. Then at the end of lesson 3, include three exercises from lesson 2 and five from the new skill learned in lesson 3. In lesson 4, bring in the remaining two problems from lesson 2, three more exercises from lesson 3, and five from the new skill learned in lesson 4. In other words, spread out your practice exercises with review exercises from prior lessons distributed throughout the course.

Another way to leverage the benefits of spaced practice is by scheduling your training in a series of virtual (synchronous) e-learning sessions. Rather than two consecutive days of face-to-face classroom training that lumps all of the practice in a short time frame, extend learning by scheduling several shorter sessions in a virtual class. For my own seminars, I have converted a two-day classroom workshop to five three-hour virtual sessions that meet every day for a week. This schedule allows practice sessions to be distributed throughout the week leading to better retention.

Evidence on distribution of practice is the basis for my next suggestion.

◆ ◆ ◆

Practice Guideline 3:

Distribute practice within your lessons and throughout your course rather than lumping them together.

◆ ◆ ◆

How to Group Practice Problems

Imagine that you are teaching how to use Excel to 1) calculate simple additions or subtractions, 2) calculate additions or subtractions combined with multiplication or division, and 3) plot the results in a graph. A traditional approach follows each topic explanation with practice problems organized by type. For example, four problems focus on additions and subtractions, then four on combinations with multiplication and division, and finally four on graphs.

This is an organizational scheme instructional psychologists call *blocking*. Each practice set is "blocked" by one specific skill. An alternative approach is to mix the practice problems. After an explanation on all three concepts, assign one practice on addition-subtraction, one on combined formulas, and one on graphs. Repeat this pattern four times. This organizational pattern is called the *mixed practice* schedule. But which plan is best for learning: blocked or mixed?

Evidence on Blocked and Mixed Practice

Rohrer and Taylor (2007) compared blocked and mixed practice in lessons that taught how to calculate the volume of four unusual shapes.

Participants received the same tutorials and practice on the four shapes over two sessions scheduled one week apart to take advantage of spaced practice. After the second session, everyone was tested. The difference between the two groups was how the tutorials and practice were grouped. The mixed group received a tutorial on all four shapes followed by practice problems that included each of the four types. The blocked group received a tutorial on shape A followed by practice on shape A. Next they received a tutorial on shape B followed by practice on shape B and so on.

The research team measured performance on both the practice problems and on the test. The results are summarized in figure 10.4.

As you can see, answers to practice problems were more accurate when they were grouped by type. Blocking makes the practice process easier.

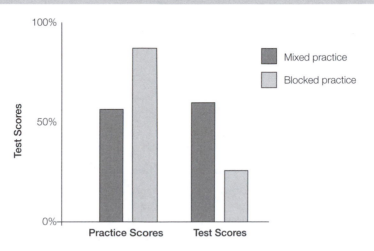

Figure 10.4. Mixed Practice Makes for Poorer Practice Scores but Better Learning

Adapted from Rohrer & Taylor, 2007.

However, did the easier practice translate into better test performance? Actually, learners in the mixed practice group showed better learning on the test than those in the blocked practice group. In other words, a more challenging practice schedule that mixed skills resulted in better learning. Hatala et al. (2003) reported similar findings when teaching medical students how to interpret ECG data. Evidence on similar versus varied context practice is the basis for my recommendation.

◆ ◆ ◆

Practice Guideline 4:

When it's important to respond differently to different categories of problems, mix practice items rather than grouping similar practice types together.

◆ ◆ ◆

As a trainer, this guideline may be a bit painful to implement. Because the classroom experience will be more difficult, you will be tempted to make things easier for learners by organizing practice in blocks according to each topic. You will need to keep in mind the paradox that a more challenging practice assignment (mixed practice) will yield better learning in the long term.

Feedback

Try a quick experiment. Close your eyes and on a piece of scratch paper draw a line that is 4 inches long. Keep your eyes closed and practice drawing five more lines that are 4 inches long. Do you think your line accuracy is better with your last attempt then at the start? Get a ruler and measure each line to see if you did get more accurate with practice.

Now repeat the experiment. Close your eyes and draw a line 4 inches long. Then open your eyes and measure your line for feedback. Is it too long or short? Close your eyes and try again. After repeating this process several times, chances are your lines will get pretty close to the target of 4 inches. This experiment was tried by American educational psychology pioneer Thorndike in the early part of the twentieth century. Not surprisingly, he found that practice with no feedback did not improve performance.

Some tasks generate *intrinsic feedback*. By that I mean, you are able to immediately experience the results of your practice attempt. A good example is practice putting in golf or entering a formula into a spreadsheet. As soon as you hit the ball you can see where it goes. When you enter the formula correctly, you get no error message and you can see the results of your calculation. If the numbers are simple enough you can even confirm the accuracy of the calculation manually.

In contrast, other tasks may not provide immediate or obvious signs of successful outcomes. A good example is learning how to input and refine search terms to locate relevant data in databases. You can input your search term and view the results. However, if you get only a few hits you won't know if it's because your term was not optimal, the databases you selected were not the best, or there are simply not many items in the databases to satisfy your search. All practice exercises benefit from feedback, but tasks that lack intrinsic feedback especially benefit from knowledge of practice results in the form of feedback.

What Is Feedback?

Feedback is information regarding the accuracy of the response to a practice attempt. It can be as simple as simply stating "right" or "incorrect" after a response. It can be as complex as a lengthy debrief of a simulated exercise in which you and others (instructor, peers) review responses and discuss them in detail. Feedback can focus on the reason a response is correct or incorrect. It can also focus not only on the outcome but on the techniques used to achieve the outcome. For example, in figure 10.5 I show feedback from an online auto troubleshooting simulation that shows the learner's steps compared with an expert's steps.

Figure 10.5. Online Feedback in a Troubleshooting Simulation

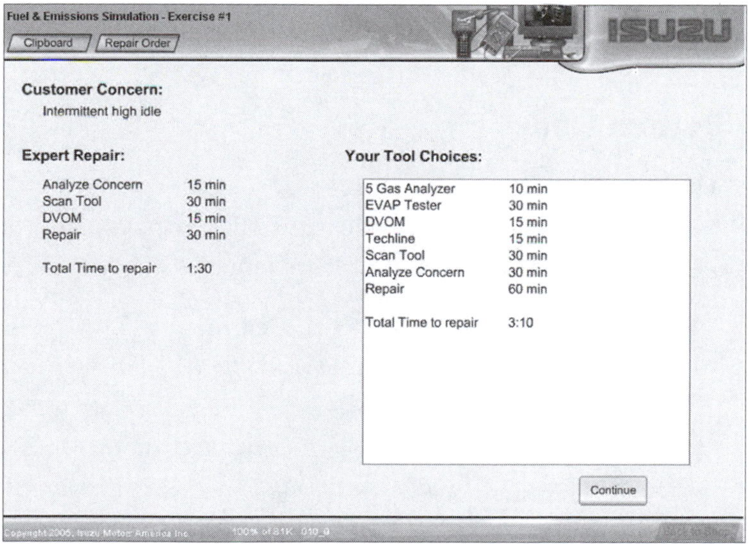

With permission from Raytheon Professional Services.

What Kind of Feedback Works Best?

The easiest kind of feedback is to simply tell learners that their responses are correct or incorrect. However, when Moreno (2004) compared this type of feedback to feedback that not only told learners whether they were right or wrong but also gave them a brief explanation, the more detailed feedback led to better learning. In a learning game that focused on botany, she found that a comment such as "Yes, in a low sunlight environment, a large leaf has more room to make food by photosynthesis" led to better learning than a response of "correct."

The evidence we have on feedback is the basis for my next recommendation.

◆ ◆ ◆

Practice Guideline 5:

Provide detailed feedback to practice exercises that explains why a response is correct or incorrect. Give feedback not only on outcomes but also on techniques and processes when appropriate to the learning goal.

◆ ◆ ◆

The Bottom Line

What Do You Think?

Now that you have reviewed the evidence, I offer my comments on the questions we considered at the start of the chapter.

- [ ] A. The more practice, the better the learning.
  TRUE. But there are some caveats. Although effective practice can lead to improved performance, the biggest skill gains accrue in the first few practice sessions. As practice continues you get diminishing returns. Maximum benefits accrue from deliberate practice that focuses on specific individual skill gaps. You will need to consider the criticality of the task and the need for automaticity as you weigh the return-on-investment of extensive practice.

- [ ] B. Six practice exercises placed at end of the lesson will lead to better learning than the same six exercises distributed throughout the lesson.

FALSE. Putting all of your practice in one spot in your lesson or course is not as good as dispersing it throughout. We have ample evidence that practice distributed throughout learning events leads to better long-term learning.

☐ C. When teaching two topics, it's better to group practice questions according to topic than to mix questions for both topics in the same session.

FALSE. Although it will make the instructional event more challenging, you will get better learning from mixed practice. If your content includes concepts and strategic skills, blend questions from the different topics to maximize learning.

☐ D. "List the five steps to construct a formula in Excel" is an effective practice exercise.

FALSE. This Excel practice item is a regurgitate question. It asks for memorization and does not require any understanding. Because the job requires actual construction of formulas, a better use of instructional time is to ask learners to create formulas.

☐ E. Learners benefit from knowing whether their answers are correct or incorrect after responding to a practice question.

TRUE, with a caveat. Knowing whether your answer is correct or incorrect is necessary but not sufficient for full learning. The best type of feedback provides an explanation for why a response is correct or incorrect, which may focus on techniques or problem-solving processes.

Applying Practice to Your Training

How can you apply the research we've reviewed in this chapter to your own learning environment? First, remember that to learn a new skill does require practice, and depending on the criticality and complexity of the task, it may require a great deal of practice. However, practice is expensive and, unless optimized, may not give you a return-on-investment. As you plan your lessons and courses, apply the following guidelines:

☐ Resist the temptation to cover more material at the expense of practice opportunities.

☐ Create practice exercises that mirror the knowledge and skills of the work environment.

☐ Avoid most regurgitation exercises that promote rote learning in favor of application exercises that incorporate the context of the job. Use job realistic scenarios as a springboard for practice questions.

☐ Adjust the amount of practice based on the criticality of the task performance and the need for automatic responses on the job.

☐ Distribute practice throughout your learning event. Take advantage of virtual learning environments to disperse practice opportunities over time.

☐ Vary the context of practice when the goal is both how to perform a skill as well as knowing when to apply that skill. As you distribute your practice sessions among lessons, mix the skills practiced and reap the benefits of spaced practice and varied context practice.

☐ Remember that practice in the absence of knowledge of outcomes fails to improve performance. Offer explanatory feedback to practice responses.

☐ Focus feedback on the outcome of the practice as well as on the process or techniques used to reach the outcome.

For More Information

Clark, R.C., & R.E. Mayer (2008b). *e-Learning & the Science of Instruction*, 2d ed. San Francisco: Pfeiffer. See ch. 11.

Clark, R.C. (2008). *Building Expertise* 3rd ed. San Francisco: Pfeiffer. See ch. 10.

Part IV

Leveraging Learning Architectures

All learning environments incorporate assumptions about learning. In this section I draw on evidence presented in the previous chapters to offer guidance on how to create learning environments based on presentations, small steps, and immersion.

◆ ◆ ◆

Giving Principled Presentations

◆ ◆ ◆

Chapter 11

Giving Principled Presentations

In conference rooms, lecture halls, training centers, and hotel meeting rooms, approximately 1.25 million PowerPoint presentations are being given *every hour* (Levasseru & Sawyer 2006)! Presentation experts estimate a waste of $250 million per day from bad PowerPoints (Paradi 2005). In the minute it takes you to read these paragraphs, there are 21,000 PowerPoint slides flooding screens around the world. How many of these presentations offer a return-on-investment?

by Ann Kwinn & C. Kwinn

The alternative to death by Power-Point is *principled presentations* that promote learning.

In this chapter we will look at how the proven guidelines reviewed through this book apply to training presentations. Specifically we will review 1) the features of principled presentations; and 2) how to plan, develop, and deliver them.

The Ubiquitous Presentation

Conferences, meetings, webinars, classroom, and e-learning lessons. Presentations are everywhere. Worldwide, presentations are the most common method for training adults (Bligh 2000). Some training events rely just about 100 percent on presentation alone. I called these *show-and-tell* lessons. Other training events include presentations as one of their instructional methods. For example, a lecture with slides might be followed by a case study and discussion. Alternatively, an asynchronous online lesson might incorporate brief narrated presentations followed by drag-and-drop online exercises.

I believe that presentations are one of the most used and abused instructional methods—often misplaced to achieve goals better attained with other training approaches. Nevertheless, I predict presentations will continue to predominate learning events—either on their own or as part of a larger instructional program. They are fast. They are easy. They can be cheap to produce and efficient to distribute via the Internet. They allow the sponsoring organization to document that the content was covered.

As long as we are going to live with presentations, let's look at how to leverage them most effectively in the service of learning. There are plenty of books and resources full of tips and techniques for presentations. Unlike these, however, I will emphasize principled presentations that incorporate research evidence into their planning, development, and delivery.

What Do You Think?

Place a check next to each statement you believe to be true about presentations:

- [ ] A. Letting the audience use handheld clickers to respond to questions during a classroom lecture will improve learning.
- [ ] B. Presentations should rely heavily on visuals.
- [ ] C. Handouts of presentation slides will help participants take notes and learn more.
- [ ] D. Presentations tend to impose more mental load than other training architectures.

What Is a Principled Presentation?

A *principled presentation* is an audio explanation by a speaker that incorporates proven modes and methods to help learners build work-relevant knowledge. The presentation can occur in a face-to-face setting such as at a conference or in a classroom. Or the presentation might be delivered in a virtual classroom or via a multimedia asynchronous lesson.

What are the key instructional modes and methods that distinguish a principled presentation from just a presentation? I summarize these in table 11.1.

1. The Presentation Goals Are Realistic

Presentations are best suited to communicate information or to build an understanding of relevant concepts or processes. Some sample topics that benefit from presentations include 1) the benefits and features of the new product line, 2) compliance with organizational policies from safety to ethics, 3) organizational structure and function for new hires, and 4) driving regulations. Don't rely on a presentation (in and of itself) to teach behavioral skills, promote critical thinking, or teach values.

Table 11.1. Six Features of Principled Presentations

Feature	Description
Realistic Goals	The presentation is designed to communicate or teach information such as facts or concepts and is NOT intended to build skills
Engaging	The presentation includes instructional methods that promote psychological processing
Visual	The presentation incorporates visuals that promote learning and avoids visuals that defeat learning
Leverages Social Presence	The presentation uses techniques appropriate to the delivery environment to engage attendees with the presenter and/or with one another
Includes Examples	The presentation incorporates examples that are relevant to the working environment of the attendees
Concise and Focused	The presentation is brief and does not maunder

2. The Presentation Is Engaging

I distinguish between two forms of engagement: *psychological* and *behavioral*. *Psychological engagement* means the learner is deeply processing the content. Psychological engagement may or may not be associated with behavioral activity. Can you think of situations in which you are behaviorally active but psychologically tuned out? Mopping the floor (an activity I should do more of) and working in my garden are two examples that come to mind for me. Conversely, during activities like reading a book we are behaviorally passive but can be very engaged mentally. Our goal in presentations is psychological engagement that can occur with or without overt behavioral responses.

Overt Engagement During Presentations. What evidence do we have that overt interactivity during presentations improves learning? Mayer, Stull et al. (2009) compared learning from three groups taking a college-level educational psychology class. One group responded to two to four questions per lecture with a remote controlled handheld clicker that recorded and then projected class responses. After viewing the group responses, the instructor led a discussion of the reasons for the correct answer. A second group (no clicker group) received the same questions but did not make any overt response. A control group attended the lectures with no questions. The clicker group gained approximately *one-third of a grade point* over the other two groups (which did not differ from one another). In this experiment, a behavioral response led to better psychological activity than just hearing questions with no response requirement. Perhaps in the no response group the questions were heard but not deeply processed since there was no overt response requirement. Active responses to relevant questions during a presentation do improve learning.

Virtual classrooms offer many more opportunities for participant involvement than face-to-face environments. As you can see in figure 11.1, the typical virtual classroom interface offers opportunities for learners to respond to questions via polling, to type chat responses and comments, to draw or write on the whiteboard, and to talk. Of course, as with any technology, presenters can ignore these features and deliver a passive presentation. The effect can be soporific. In response, the audience can and will easily and unobtrusively minimize the virtual classroom window and turn to other activities.

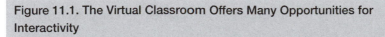

Figure 11.1. The Virtual Classroom Offers Many Opportunities for Interactivity

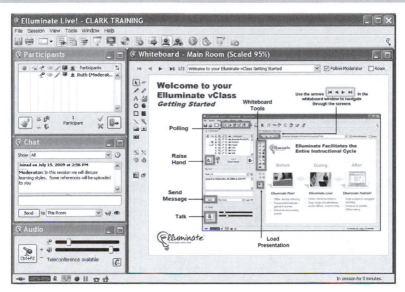

Psychological Activity During Presentations. There are some presentations devoid of behavioral interactivity that are still effective for learning. In these situations your presentation promotes psychological processing in the absence of behavioral responses. Factual presentations that are brief and targeted to an experienced audience motivated to learn the content can be effective even without overt audience response. For example, medical residents rated a standard one-hour lecture higher than a more interactive session that included discussion (Haidet et al. 2004). Furthermore, learning was about the same from both versions. The medical residents had sufficient context and interest to process the content of the lecture with or without overt activity.

In summary, a well-organized noninteractive presentation that uses engagement methods such as visuals or rhetorical questions can be effective in brief time frames when targeted to an experienced and focused audience.

3. The Presentation Is Visual

A recent conference I attended required participants to download their own handouts. As I browsed through the posted materials I was surprised to find that the majority of them were PowerPoint walls of words—no visuals! I reviewed solid evidence in chapters 5 and 8 regarding the power of visuals to promote learning. A useful visual is one that shows the relationships among ideas in the presentation. For example, a visual agenda in the form of a hierarchical chart (shown in figure 11.2) can establish the presentation framework during the introduction and can keep the audience oriented as the presentation moves from one topic to the next.

Figure 11.2. An Organizational Visual Communicates the Presentation Agenda

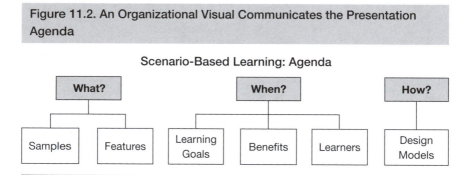

4. The Presentation Leverages Social Presence

Social presence arises from communication between the audience and the speaker as well as among audience members. The presenter should invite social presence by looking and sounding "approachable" rather than "on a pedestal." An "available" instructor is one of the features of any learning event shown to correlate with higher course ratings (Sitzmann et al. 2008) and with better learning (Mayer 2009). A win–win! Specifically, the presenter should use a conversational tone and language, smile and maintain eye contact in a physical setting, reveal his or her own opinions or experiences relevant to the content, invite questions and comments, and encourage interactions among the attendees such as brief buzz groups. In short, audience ratings and learning will be higher when the presenter is a learning host. A good hostess makes her guests feel comfortable with herself and with other guests.

5. The Presentation Includes Examples

We saw the power of examples to accelerate expertise in chapter 9. For maximum effect make your examples interactive. You could start your presentation with an example (or nonexample) and ask the attendees to rate or discuss it. In figure 11.3, I show a slide from a presentation I make on evidence-based e-learning. The screen shot links to a brief multimedia lesson that violates most of the major guidelines of my presentation. I show this counter-example demonstration during my introduction and ask attendees to grade it and to discuss their grade in a small group. In a large face-to-face session, the discussion takes place in small buzz groups and in a virtual session, participants talk in virtual breakout rooms or use chat.

Figure 11.3. A Counter Example Serves as a Kickoff Activity

Grade this sample: A to F

Show examples not only at the beginning but also throughout your presentation. Examples establish relevance, are concrete, and serve as bridges from the content to the brains of participants. Maximize the benefit of your examples by asking participants to respond them. See chapter 9 for ways to make your examples interactive.

6. The Presentation Is Concise and Focused

I recall hearing a conference attendee in the elevator after my presentation on cognitive load theory. He was unaware that I was one of the many in the crowd on their way to the next session. "Gosh," he said, "I don't really know what she said, but I know it's really important stuff!" When I reviewed my hour-long presentation I realized that my 120-slide lecture was way too ambitious for the time frame and the attendees. Like a typical subject matter expert, I had tried to squeeze in just about everything I knew about cognitive load theory. And in the process I violated my presentation theme by overloading my participants! Over time, I've gotten more disciplined in my presentations and in my writing as well, by weeding out extra topics, tossing irrelevant examples and stories, and skipping or adapting activities that are too ambitious for the time allotted. Rather than "cheating" attendees, I do them a favor when I implement the less is more principle.

Creating the Principled Presentation

A successful principled presentation is the offspring of 60 percent planning and development prior to the event, 20 percent delivery proficiency, and 20 percent environmental and situation-specific factors such as the setting, the audience, technology glitches, and so on.

I could write a whole book on the details associated with each of these phases. But others have already done that. Instead, I summarize common presentation problems in the three key phases of presentation development: 1) planning the presentation; 2) developing the presentation slides, speaker notes, and handouts; and 3) delivering the presentation.

What Can Go Wrong at the Planning Phase

Planning involves translating upfront research and reflection regarding the intended purpose of your presentation, features of your audience and speaking environment into a presentation structure and approach. Some common problems that emerge from incomplete or inaccurate planning include the following.

Wrong Goals for a Presentation

Have you ever tried to achieve goals in a presentation that would have been better achieved by other instructional methods? Your sponsor may impose outcome presentation goals that are better trained with a hands-on session. For example, presentations are useful to communicate knowledge but fall short for skill building or motivational outcomes. When you are faced with inappropriate requests from sponsors, respond by offering other more appropriate training alternatives. My colleague Chopeta Lyons has a great response to clients with ill-advised requests: "Yes, I can do that. But I would be remiss if I did not tell you. . . ."(and she continues to explain why their approach won't be as effective as an alternative).

Goals Don't Fit Audience or Time Frame

Are your goals too ambitious (or too watered down) for the time allotted and the audience? I told you about my overly detailed presentation on cognitive load theory—too many details, too many slides for a one-hour presentation. By the way, I've seen the opposite as well—underdeveloped presentations that had too little meat for the time frame and audience.

Irrelevant Goals

Will your presentation goals be relevant to the audience's context or background? Irrelevant presentation goals got me fired! I was commissioned by a medical equipment manufacturer to teach a one-day session on the psychology of learning and evidence-based training methods. The audience was field staff, primarily salespeople who also had collateral training duties. I had asked them to bring a sample lesson with them, thinking that reviewing their samples would make the session relevant. When I asked for a show of hands as to who had brought a lesson with them, guess what? Not one! The presentation bombed completely. Those folks had not the slightest interest in learning psychology or training techniques.

I soon abandoned my presentation plan and asked the participants to meet in groups and list their main training challenges. My goal was to respond to their agenda rather than force mine. But this activity resulted in lists of complaints about how the central training staff (my sponsors) made their lives miserable. Things went downhill from there. It was a classic no-win situation that could have been avoided with better upfront analysis and planning.

As you reflect on your goals and audience, consider an organizing framework as well as what kinds of activities you may want to include. I summarize three common presentation frameworks in figure 11.4 that can be conflated to fit your purposes.

Once you have a high-level plan, it's time to start developing the core elements of an effective presentation: slides and handouts. This puts you in the development phase.

What Can Go Wrong at the Development Phase

Now your presentation plan comes to life. You are creating slides, writing handouts, jotting down talking points. Development is the incarnation of your planning phase. At this stage you will confront many questions. How many slides to produce? Should you have a handout? If yes, what type? What kinds of presenter notes to develop? Here's some common development missteps.

Death by PowerPoint

How many slides should you develop for your presentation? Presentations such as classroom lectures or webinars are paced by the presenter—not the learners. Consequently, presentations run greater risk of causing

Figure 11.4. Organizational Schemes for Presentations

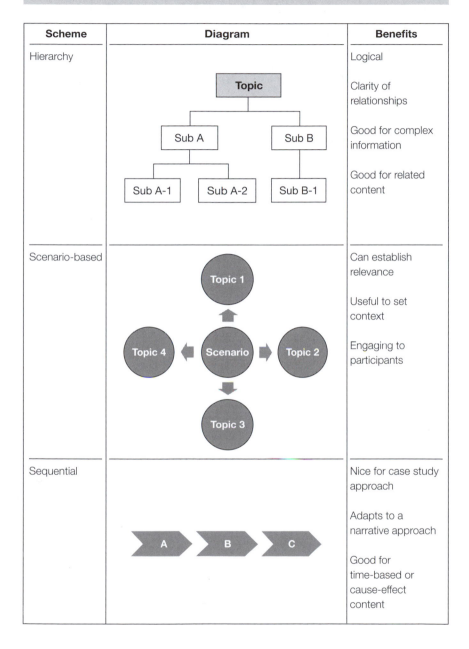

Scheme	Diagram	Benefits
Hierarchy		Logical Clarity of relationships Good for complex information Good for related content
Scenario-based		Can establish relevance Useful to set context Engaging to participants
Sequential		Nice for case study approach Adapts to a narrative approach Good for time-based or cause-effect content

mental overload than self-paced media such as books or asynchronous e-learning. Too many complex slides can overload. Alternatively, too few slides can fail to sustain attention due to lack of visual interest and stagnation.

I know of no evidence supporting any specific metric for numbers of slides. In my own presentations I average one slide per minute. So for an hour conference session, I'll typically develop 55–65 slides. This does not mean I show one slide every minute. During a short activity a single slide might remain in place for several minutes. During an explanation, I might have six slides for one topic and two for another. In contrast, I've heard really great keynote presentations based on maybe 10 or 12 slides. You will need to consider the complexity of the topic, the background and size of your audience as well as the delivery media and setting. A keynote for 500 will benefit from a different solution than a smaller presentation for 15.

No Visual Interest

The worst case? No visuals at all. There are no slides or the slides are walls of words. There are a few talented speakers who can command and sustain attention through their voice alone. But for the purpose of learning, even a talented speaker can get a better result by using effective visuals. Be visual from the start. I recommend a title slide that uses a visual to generate interest, arouse curiosity, and convey the purpose of the session.

Handouts

By handout I refer to a physical, usually print-based, guide given to participants at the start of a presentation. There are many options for handouts, and in table 11.2 I summarize the benefits and drawbacks of the most common alternatives. Until recently, most often handouts were printouts of the presentation slides. In the last few years, many conference organizers have requested different formats. For example, rather than pages of slides, they request a brief text summary, references, and

Table 11.2. Common Formats for Presentation Handouts

Format	Benefits	Drawbacks
Slides	1) Participants like them 2) Easy for speaker to prepare 3) Keep participants oriented	1) Will require participant note taking 2) Can waste a lot of paper if hardcopy 3) Usually poor reference resource
Text Outline	1) Easy for speaker to prepare 2) Provides an organizer 3) Consumes less paper if hardcopy	1) Generally less popular than slides 2) Will require participant note taking 3) Usually a poor reference resource
Detailed Notes	1) Minimizes note taking 2) Provides a useful reference	1) More work for presenter 2) Can consume a lot of paper if hardcopy 3) Participants may get lost in presentation
Mixed: Slides + Text	1) Popular 2) Can be useful reference 3) Minimizes note taking 4) Guides participants	1) More work for presenter 2) Can consume a lot of paper if hardcopy
Article	1) Popular 2) Can be useful for reference 3) Easy for speaker if already published	1) Usually lacks correspondence with presentation so audience gets lost 2) Can consume a lot of paper if hardcopy

a job aid to help attendees apply the ideas of the presentation after the event.

There is no single best handout, but I do feel that in general handouts of slides alone are not optimal. Slides alone will encourage note taking and in many situations lead to split attention. Slides alone are incomplete and don't usually make good references. Rather than slides alone, define your handout based on the goals, constraints, and audience features you defined during planning.

What Can Go Wrong at the Delivery Phase

Imagine that you have invested sufficient time and effort to planning and developing. You have a solid presentation. However, at show time it's up to the speaker to make it come alive. What can go wrong the day and hour of the event?

Death by Speaker Introduction

Well-intended event hosts can take up to 15 minutes of your allotted speaking time with various housekeeping, acknowledgement, and marketing duties as well as with a lengthy speaker introduction often read word for word. I usually ask my host to let me make my own introduction trying to limit them to less than a minute. Keep your personal introduction very succinct. No one is that interested at the start of a presentation about your organization, its products, your detailed educational history, your grandchildren, and so on. I recommend just a single slide to establish your credibility and enthusiasm for the topic. As the presentation evolves, you can insert information about yourself and in that way evolve a more natural relationship throughout your session.

Audience Confusion

Will your attendees immediately get what the presentation is about, what it might accomplish, or how it will be organized? If not, they have no framework, and no basis for deciding if it's relevant to their needs. Confusion may be the result of a divagating presentation with insufficient structure or failure to communicate the structure to the audience.

Technical Glitches

You know the saying: What can go wrong will. Technology can let you down. First, I recommend using your own computer and double checking that your computer has the needed capacity and software for your presentation. Bring a second copy of your presentation on a memory stick as a backup. Second, insist on a rehearsal prior to the event. Test everything. Third, don't include unreliable technology as part of your event. Even to this day I shy away from drawing on the Internet as a critical part of my presentation. Connectivity in the presentation room may be poor or the Internet may go down. At a minimum, have a backup of essential screen captures. Fourth, always have a plan B for critical elements of your presentation. If a multimedia presentation fails, go to backup screen captures or substitute a different multimedia presentation. When giving virtual classroom sessions, I always send the event producer a copy of my slides and make a paper copy for myself. That way if you lose connectivity (it's happened to me more than once), you can ask the sponsor to load the slides and continue your presentation referencing a paper copy.

Derailment

Have you ever been thrown off your presentation plan? It's easy to deviate from your plan during the actual presentation. Maundering speakers and audience questions are two common culprits. Disciplined planning and development should help. I usually print out thumbnails of my slides and write time guidelines in them. For example, I mark the slide where I should be at half my time. I believe in inviting audience questions during the presentation in most cases. It's part of being a good host. And it helps you see where you are or are not connecting. The trick is to use your responses to audience questions to forward your presentation agenda by adding an example, clarifying, or briefly discussing a different facet of your topic. Often you can use audience questions to jump start your next point.

The Inflexible Speaker

I told you about my presentation from hell. I should have abandoned my presentation plan right away and asked the participants what they would like to know or do. Most situations are not that dire. The most common problem is time—often too little time for your agenda. I always have some optional slides as part of my presentation. If I get questions or an activity takes longer than anticipated, I skip them. I do try to stick to 80 percent plus of my agenda, which has usually been published ahead and presented as part of the introduction. But good planning leaves your presentation scalable—you can skip some of the detail without short-changing your agenda.

No Social Presence

You know all of this stuff already. If you can arrive early, take advantage of the wait time to meet and greet your attendees. Smile. It's simple, but speakers are often nervous or concentrating on their performance and forget to smile and look the audience in the eye. Use a conversational approach. Don't read a script. Build up passion for your topics—it will come through in your voice, words, and body language. Finally, never "take on" an audience member who voices a disagreement with your topics. Always thank them for their contribution and respond with either a clarification or a noncommittal statement such as "Well, that's another way to look at it," or "Hmm, it would be interesting to test out that idea."

The Bottom Line

What Do You Think?

Now that you have reviewed the evidence, below are my comments on the following questions:

- ☐ A. Letting the audience use clickers to respond to questions during a classroom lecture will improve learning.
  TRUE. Using clickers is one technique proven to promote learning during a lecture. There are many others that you can consider such as show of hands, buzz sessions, polling, and chat in virtual settings.
- ☐ B. Presentations should rely heavily on visuals.
  TRUE. We have lots of evidence that relevant visuals can promote learning and participants like them.
- ☐ C. Handouts of presentation slides will help participants take notes and learn more.
  MAYBE NOT. Handouts should help reduce divided attention caused by extensive note taking and should also provide a useful reference resource. Rather than a printout of the slides, however, consider a job aid with a checklist or a table that summarizes the main facts and concepts.

☐ D. Presentations tend to impose more mental load than other training architectures.

TRUE. Because presentations are paced by the presenter, they can easily over load the audience—more so than a self-paced environment where the learners can go at their own rate.

Quality Assurance Checklist

☐ The speaker has arrived early and tested the technology.

☐ The speaker has a plan B.

☐ The speaker has arrived early and greets the attendees.

☐ The introduction is visual and immediately communicates the relevance and road map for the event.

☐ More than 75 percent of the slides include relevant visuals.

☐ The pacing is brisk enough to hold attention.

☐ The audience remains oriented to the topics and road map.

☐ Activities are suitable to the time frame, purpose, audience, and technology.

☐ The speaker invites social presence through a conversational approach, informal body language, and responses to questions.

☐ The goals of the presentation are realistic and achievable within the time frame allowed.

☐ Handouts help the participants follow the presentation logic and provide follow-up information as a job aid or references.

For More Information

Bligh, D.A. (2000). *What's the Use of Lectures?* San Francisco: Jossey-Bass.

Clark, R.C. (2008). *Building Expertise*, 3d ed. San Francisco: Pfeiffer. See ch. 9.

Clark, R.C., & A. Kwinn (2007). *The New Virtual Classroom*. San Francisco: Pfeiffer.

Clark, R.C., & R.E. Mayer (2008a). "Learning by viewing versus learning by doing: Evidence-based guidelines for principled learning environments." *Performance Improvement* 47, 5–13.

◆ ◆ ◆

Building Stair-Step Lessons

◆ ◆ ◆

Chapter 12

Building Stair-Step Lessons

1. Give the learner immediate feedback.

2. Break down the task into small steps.

3. Repeat the directions as many times as possible.

4. Work from the most simple to the most complex tasks.

5. Give positive reinforcement.

—Wikipedia

by Ann Kwinn & C. Kwinn

These instructional prescriptions from B.F. Skinner, the father of Behaviorist Psychology, are the historical foundation from which stair-step learning architectures of today grow.

In this chapter I draw on proven guidelines reviewed through the book to apply them to stair-step architecture lessons. Specifically, we will review 1) the components of effective stair-step lessons, and 2) what can go wrong.

Are Stair-Step Lessons *Not* Cool?

The training community is focusing on hot topics like social media, mobile learning, and serious games. Since you rarely hear about them, you might infer that traditional stair-step or part-task training approaches are obsolete. After all, their roots are in behaviorist approaches to learning fashionable over 50 years ago. Traditional building block courses are often ignored or perceived as boring or irrelevant to today's training needs. Stair-step lessons have even been labeled "Simon Says" training. You might be surprised to know that there is solid evidence for the learning benefits of stair-step designs for the right audience and learning goals.

Stair-step designs are most appropriate when teaching novice learners how to perform tasks that are primarily procedural. They work well for content that can be segmented and sequenced in a prerequisite order. Content such as mathematics and much software training—in fact any task with logical sequences—adapts well to a stair-step approach.

A stair-step lesson begins by teaching the key knowledge topics needed to perform the task and ends with teaching the task steps. The lessons are chunked into short topics, each followed by a practice exercise with feedback. Stair-step lessons are very instructive, are highly guided, and use an instructional pattern of "tell . . . show . . . practice . . . feedback."

What Do You Think?

Place a check next to each statement you believe is true about stair-step lessons:

- ☐ A. Learning is better when topics are presented in small chunks.
- ☐ B. Learning is better when related knowledge content is sequenced prior to lesson task content.
- ☐ C. Handouts should not be provided for stair-step lessons.
- ☐ D. Stair-step lessons can be presented in classrooms or asynchronous e-learning.
- ☐ E. Learning is better when practice exercises are distributed throughout stair-step lessons.

The Anatomy of a Stair-Step Lesson

An effective stair-step lesson includes a highly guided series of short topics with practice for each topic concluding with a final lesson task or task(s). Stair-step lessons can be effectively designed for classroom or e-learning both synchronous and asynchronous. In this chapter I use a classroom example to illustrate a stair-step lesson architecture. However, the same techniques of "tell, show, try-it, and correct" work fine in multimedia lessons. Because the "tell and show" parts of the lesson are usually delivered by an instructor presentation in the classroom, many of the techniques I described in the previous chapter on presentations apply to stair-step lessons as well.

I divide stair-step lessons into three main parts: 1) introduction, 2) supporting topics with practice and feedback, and 3) lesson task with practice and feedback.

1. Lesson Introduction

The lesson introduction is critical to set the stage for learning. Don't short-change it. You need to accomplish several goals that I illustrate in my Excel sample lesson handout in figure 12.1. First, learners need to know the anticipated outcome and road map of the lesson. I use the learning objectives and lesson overview for this purpose. Second, the learners need to see the relevance and work-related context for what they are about to learn. For my sample Excel lesson, I kick off with a simple instructor demonstration illustrating how a formula automatically updates calculation results when spreadsheet data is changed. A good technique for the relevance and context portion of the introduction is to show the benefits of the lesson skills in a work setting. This can be through a "what went wrong" or a "what went right" demonstration, scenario, video, or data. Third, the introduction should activate relevant prior knowledge stored in long-term memory. This can be accomplished by starting the lesson with some review questions from prior lessons, presenting an analogy, or initiating a discussion about problems participants face related to the learning goal. For example, in a new supervisor's class, a short group discussion can generate a list of problems participants have faced with employee performance.

The introduction should be concise, informative, and engaging. The learners should exit knowing the outcomes and road map, appreciating the relevance of the skills to their work and aware of related prior knowledge.

2. The Supporting Topics

One of the key design features of a stair-step architecture is sequencing the main *supporting topics prior to* the steps to perform a task. As you can see in the order of topics at the bottom of figure 12.1, the Excel lesson teaches two main topics: cell references and formula formats prior to the tasks of entering a formula and creating a chart. Most main supporting topics are "What Is It" content along with any facts related to that topic. "What Is It" knowledge is best taught by tell (give an explanation), show (give some examples), followed by practice (identify a valid example from samples or produce a valid example), and feedback.

In figures 12.2 and 12.3 you can see the handout pages for the "What Is It" lesson topic: formula formats. The explanation summarizes the key elements of a formula. The three examples incorporate all of the elements in various legal combinations. Remember from chapter 9, I recommended adding questions to examples to ensure their processing. I use that technique here in the section labeled "Format Questions" in figure 12.2. The goal of these questions is to encourage learners to review the examples carefully and induce some critical rules such as "all formulas begin with an equal sign." Following the tell-and-show sections, I added some important rules (facts) about order of operations along with a mnemonic to help recall the correct sequence.

Figure 12.1. An Introductory Page in an Excel Training Manual

Using Excel

Lesson 2
Using Formulas in Excel

Introduction

In this lesson you will apply the power of Excel formulas allowing fast and accurate updates to your spreadsheets

Importance

Have you ever added a long column of numbers only to have to change one number and then recalculate the whole column? Watch the demonstration to see how an Excel formula can save you time with automatic updates!

Lesson Overview

In this lesson we will learn to use formulas and graph the results of the calculations. Along the way you will learn to:

1. Use cell references,
2. Format formulas to achieve calculation goals,
3. Input formulas into the spreadsheet
4. Create bar and pie charts for your results.

Lesson Objective

You will input the correct formula to achieve calculation goals and graph the results

Order of Topics

This lesson includes the following topics.

Topic	See Page
Cell references	4
Exercise 2-1: Name that cell	5
Formula formats	6
Exercise 2-2: Using formulas	7
How to enter a formula	8
Exercise 2-3: Enter formulas	9
How to create a charts and graphs	10
Exercise 2-4: Create charts for your data	

Figure 12.2. Handout for Excel Supporting Topic on Formulas

Using Excel

Formula Formats

Parts	Excel formulas can include the following elements: • equal sign (required) • cell references • operators (+, -, *, /) • numbers • parentheses
Examples	= C3 + D6 – (E 9 + 6) = E4*B3/12 = A3/B4*G5
Format Questions	Look at the samples above: 1. How do all formulas start? 2. There are 4 possible operators. What does each mean: + means - means * means / means 3. What is the result of the second equation if E4 has a value of 4 and B3 has a value of 6?
Order of Operations	= A3*B4/D2+ 3 When A3 = 2 B4 = 3 D2 = 4 Does this mean 6 divided by 7 OR 2 times 3/7?
Clue	Use this clue to help you remember the order of operations: PDMAS: Prices Drop Most at Sales First calculations: Any elements in parentheses Second calculation: Divisions Third calculation: Multiplication Fourth calculation: Addition Fifth calculation: Subtractions

Figure 12.3. Practice for Excel Supporting Topic on Formulas

Using Excel

Exercise 1-2: Using Formulas

Directions   Using the values in the spreadsheet below, answer the formula questions below:

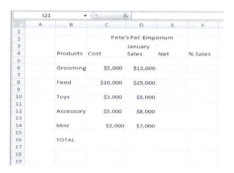

Questions   1. What is the numeric result of the following formulas:

A.   = D6 – C6

B.   = D5*C14/C6

C.   = (C6 – C14)/C10

2. Write the correct formula to calculate:

A. Total sales for January

B. Net sales for toys for January

C. Percentage of total sales from feed

Exercise 1-2 (shown in figure 12.3) asks learners to use spreadsheet cell values to manually calculate formula outcomes as well as to construct some formulas to achieve assigned formula goals. This exercise requires learners to apply an understanding of how formulas work—not just parrot back the information given in the tell-and-show sections. In the classroom, the instructor allocates a few minutes to the exercise and when she sees that most are finished, asks pairs of participants to compare their answers and resolve any discrepancies. The instructor then shows all correct answers and answers any questions. While participants are working on the exercise, the instructor moves around the room checking for any misconceptions and helping individuals as needed.

Evidence for Sequencing Supporting Topics First. What evidence do we have for the learning benefits of sequencing the supporting knowledge prior to the major lesson task? Mayer, Mathias, & Wetzell (2002) created two lesson versions on how brakes work. One version gave a multimedia stage-by-stage explanation of how brakes work. A second version included the same explanation but preceded it by a short description of each part as illustrated in figure 12.4. Learners who received the part explanations before the full description scored higher on a problem-solving test with a high effect size of .9.

Figure 12.4. A Topics-First Lesson Begins with an Explanation of Each Part

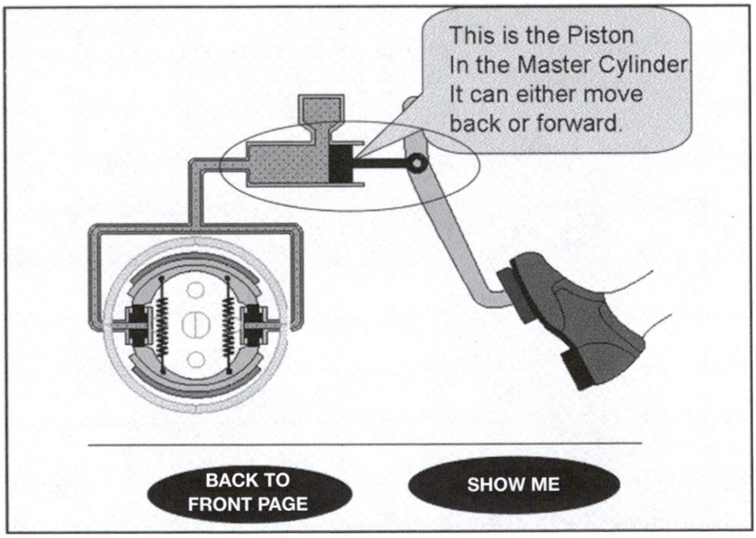

From Mayer, Mathias, and Wetzell, 2002.

In lessons that fold all of the knowledge topics into one meaty explanation, the learner is barraged with a great deal of information all at once. By teaching key concepts first, the amount of new information the learner must acquire all at once is greatly reduced. This approach helps mitigate mental overload.

Teach Supporting Topics in Context. To help learners connect the relationships between the parts and the whole, always teach supporting topics in the context of the whole task. For example, in figure 12.4, each individual part is explained in a visual that shows the structure of the entire brake. Likewise, in figure 12.3, the formula practice exercise makes use of a spreadsheet example. If you teach a series of supporting topics out of context, you end up with fragmented knowledge and confusion as to how each topic relates to the lesson task. *what it looks like now*

3. The Lesson Task

So far we have seen how to develop the lesson introduction followed by the key supporting topics. The next part of the lesson uses tell, show, and try it to teach the lesson task, which is typically a procedural task. As an example, figure 12.5 shows a handout from our sample Excel lesson. The main instructional method for teaching tasks is a follow-along demonstration given by the instructor. For reference purposes, the learner benefits from a documented summary of the steps. The best documentation during initial learning includes a visual of the work interface (screen or equipment) with text explanations placed close to the relevant portion of the visual. For tasks that will be repeated many times in training and on the job, a short working aid using text alone may suffice. For tasks that are more infrequent, a more detailed working aid with visuals to illustrate each step will make a better reference.

Practice in Stair-Step Lessons

Following an interactive demonstration, practice exercises require learners to apply the same steps to some new scenarios. Figure 12.6 shows the practice for the Excel lesson. This practice illustrates a spiral technique in which the formulas written out in exercise 2-2 are reused in exercise 2-3.

Figure 12.5. Handout for Excel Lesson Procedure

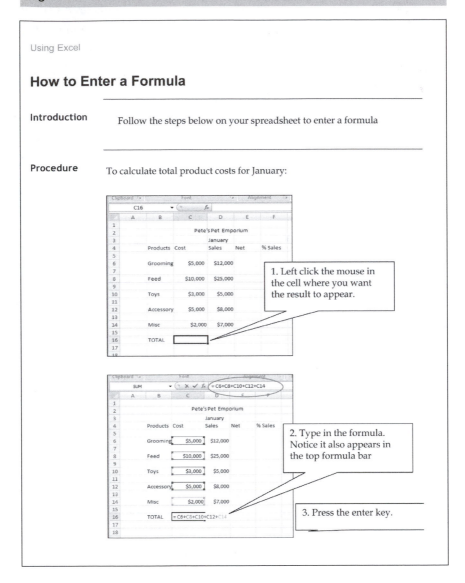

In part two of this practice, the benefit of formulas is reinforced by asking learners to change data values in the spreadsheet and document the results. Practice exercises may be initially completed alone and answers compared with class partners.

Figure 12.6. Practice Assignment for Excel Lesson Task

Using Excel

Exercise 2-3: Enter Formulas

Part 1:

Directions

Use the formulas you developed in Exercise 1-2 and enter them into your spreadsheet. Write the answers below:

A. Total sales for January

B. Net sales for toys for January

C. Percentage of total sales from feed

Part 2

Make the following data changes and recalculate the results above:

Feed sales are $30,000

Toy costs increase $1000

During the exercise, the instructor moves around the room checking on progress and giving assistance as needed. At the end of the exercise, the instructor can give feedback by simply stating the answers or if she noted confusion during the exercise, demonstrating how to obtain the results.

In some situations, workers must be able to perform a job task quickly and accurately without benefit of a working aid. Use *drill and practice* exercises in these situations. Drill and practice requires learners to perform the procedure many times until it becomes automatic. Computer simulations are useful for these types of practice exercises because the computer program can measure both accuracy and speed of response.

Handouts and Slides for Stair-Step Lessons

Evidence is mixed about the learning value of taking notes. No doubt potential benefits depend on the rate of content delivery, note taking skills, as well as familiarity with the content. Marsh and Sink (2009) found that students preferred receiving handouts and learning was better when handouts were provided. Rather than devoting attention to taking notes, learners can process the tell-and-show parts of the training and invest mental resources in practice exercises. Because training time tends to be very limited I recommend providing relatively detailed handouts—at least when the content is stable and the quality and consistency of the training is important.

There are many formats for handouts. I prefer Information Mapping™ form of structured writing illustrated in figures 12.1–12.3 and 12.5–12.6. Structured writing techniques have historically been used for documentation purposes, but I find they adapt well to build training handouts.

When the content is volatile or development time constraints preclude detailed notes, at a minimum provide slide handouts as well as job aids for procedures. I show an example of a job aid for the Excel lesson in figure 12.7.

Figure 12.7. A Job Aid for the Excel Lesson

FORMULAS

- Start with equal sign
- Operators: + – * /
- Order of operations: PDMAS

Examples:

= A3 + B4/C6
= A3? (B4–D8)

ENTERING FORMULAS

1. Enter data in cells
2. Right click in cell where result should appear
3. Type in formula
4. Press Enter key

Figure 12.8. An Introductory Slide for the Excel Lesson

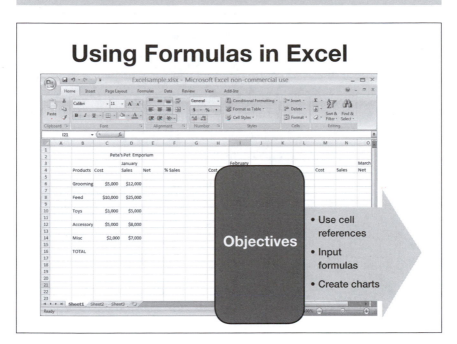

Build slides that coordinate with the handouts. Each slide includes key points and relevant visuals from the handout. For the Excel introductory page shown in figure 12.1, I would build at least three slides: a title slide shown in figure 12.8, an agenda slide, and a demonstration slide.

What Can Go Wrong with Stair-Step Lessons?

As with any training approach, things can go wrong that degrade the learning potential of the event. Remember that the most expensive element in any training program is the time participants are away from the job. Shortchanging the instructional environment may save some money in the short run but can be exponentially expensive across the delivery landscape. Here is a list of common shortfalls in stair-step lessons.

How to implement CAMBEA in your daily practice

Missing Job Context

The basic goal of stair-step courses is to teach procedural tasks along with the associated knowledge needed to perform those tasks. Most of the lessons should be rooted in a task such as How to Create an Excel Formula, How to Assemble the Erylitizer, How to Troubleshoot the Cam Loader, How to Verify the Customer's Credit. To ensure job context, conduct a job analysis to identify and segment the core tasks associated with a work role. Without a pervasive and accurate job context, the lessons will seem (and may be) irrelevant to your learners.

A common dilemma involves building lessons such as software training intended for a broad audience with diverse work roles. In this situation, define the most common tasks to be performed by users and create scenarios to illustrate and practice those tasks. To customize the training, require participants to complete a project in which they apply the skills to their own work-related data. In the Excel course, I created a demonstration and practice spreadsheet based on Pete's Pet Emporium. I could ensure learning transfer by asking participants to apply their Excel skills to a work-related project such as preparing a budget.

Suboptimal Sequencing and Segmenting

Sometimes stair-step lessons get out of control by mushrooming beyond the learner's attention span and working memory capacity. At the other end of the spectrum, you can overdo segmenting by creating lessons that are too small to be meaningful and then become tedious. There are always exceptions, but for e-learning aim for lessons about 5–10 minutes in length and classroom lessons including practice opportunities should not exceed an hour.

A common sequencing mistake is to place most of the main knowledge topics into one of the first lessons in a course in the form of a "technical terminology" lesson. This approach is usually quite boring and fails to teach the terms in the job context. Most of the knowledge topics should be placed in the same lesson that teaches a specific task, usually sequenced just prior to the actual task. In the Excel formula lesson, the knowledge topics "what is a valid formula" and "cell references" are sequenced prior to the procedure of how to enter a formula.

As you plan your instructional sequence, consider not only the content placement but also the diversity of learning events. For example, follow a short presentation with a practice or case study. When it's time for debriefs, select one or two student products to review rather than five or more at once. Interweave individual assignments with pair collaboration as well as small group work. Get participants to move around for various learning events by joining different teams, working on wall charts, and so on.

Ineffective Practice

Frequent practice with feedback is one of the core features of the stair-step architecture. Practice failures range from little or no practice (we just don't have time—we have to cover the material) to regurgitate practice that asks learners to parrot back what they have been told or read. Remember from chapter 10 that it's better to distribute practice exercises within a lesson and among lessons than to lump them all in one place. Also practice without feedback is of little value. Feedback should go beyond "right or wrong" to provide an explanation or focus on techniques that will improve performance. In classroom settings, use feedback techniques that do not threaten learner morale. For example, show a slide with correct responses and give a verbal explanation, focus feedback on the solution process (not the individual), ask pairs to review work and give each other feedback, and move around the room during practice sessions offering individualized feedback.

Ineffective Pacing

Years of classroom instruction have shown me that it is just about impossible to maintain an optimal pace for all. One of the drawbacks of the classroom is instructor pacing rather than learner pacing. No matter what, you will be too slow for some and too fast for others. I tend to pace my presentations on the fast side because I give participants a complete reference handout and I want to invest time in practice opportunities that drive learning.

Some techniques to optimize pacing include the following: 1) assign pre-work to realign a diverse background audience to a more homogeneous group, 2) have participants work or debrief together, 3) include extra "bonus" assignments for fast finishers, 4) have an ongoing background project that fast finishers can work on while others complete assignments, 5) get pacing feedback from your learners early in the event, and 6) be flexible. Flexibility means setting your instructional priorities ahead of time and skipping lower priority content or activities.

A recent virtual classroom session I led had a large class size, and we soon fell behind the planned schedule. I adjusted the design by collapsing two breakout room exercises into one and skipping a section of content in lieu of more case study work on a skill set I considered more important for the particular group. In a different instructor-led class, I was surprised to find that many of the trainers attending did not know the difference between a recall practice and an application practice. I abandoned my agenda completely to have each individual post an application practice on a wall chart. A gallery tour identified any remaining recall exercises, and the class worked collaboratively to revise them to application level.

Failure to Connect

Student ratings and learning are enhanced by a social connection between the instructor and the learners. Besides the opening introductions and greetings, one of the best times to connect is during practice exercises and case work. Often instructors are reluctant to move into the learner's space while they are working when in fact, these times offer such a great opportunity to verify that participants are getting it, catch misconceptions, and establish relationships with individual participants.

The Bottom Line

What Do You Think?

Now that we have reviewed the evidence, here are my comments:

☐ A. Learning is better when topics are presented in small chunks.
TRUE. By chunking the content and sequencing key knowledge topics first, you avoid mental overload. It's important, however, that each topic reflect the work context so the learner can see its relationship to the lesson task.

☐ B. Learning is better when related knowledge content is sequenced prior to lesson task content.
TRUE. Same comments as under A.

☐ C. Handouts should not be provided for stair-step lessons.
FALSE. Handouts are a situation-specific decision. For example, an effective online or print reference guide may preclude the need for a detailed lesson handout. Likewise, highly volatile content or short development time frames might prohibit detailed handouts. At the least, provide either a paper-based or online working aid that can help ensure transfer after learning.

☐ D. Stair-step lessons can be presented in classrooms or asynchronous e-learning.
TRUE. The architecture of a course or lesson is not really about the delivery media. It's about the basic features of the lesson including chunking and sequencing decisions.

☐ E. Learning is better when practice exercises are distributed throughout stair-step lessons
TRUE. We saw in chapter 10 that spaced practice results in better retention learning than massed practice.

Quality Assurance Checklist

☐ The stair-step architecture is used for procedural tasks and/or novice learners.

☐ Most lessons focus on a task plus associated knowledge topics.

☐ Content is segmented into short topics followed by practice with feedback.

☐ Knowledge topics are sequenced prior to task steps.

☐ The work context of the lesson is salient in the introduction and throughout the lesson.

☐ Lessons follow a tell–show–try it–feedback–correct pattern.

☐ Explanations use visuals described by audio.

☐ Examples (including demonstrations) are varied and interactive.

☐ Practices are at an application level and distributed throughout the lesson.

☐ Practices provide explanatory feedback.

☐ Handouts include working aids at a minimum.

☐ Instructors build and sustain learning relationships with the participants.

For More Information

Clark, R.C. (2008). *Developing Technical Training*, 3d ed. San Francisco: Pfeiffer.

◆ ◆ ◆

Building Immersive Learning Environments

◆ ◆ ◆

Chapter 13

Building Immersive Learning Environments

"We learn geology the morning after the earthquake."

—Ralph Waldo Emerson

Being plunged into an unfamiliar problem or situation creates a moment of need for learning. When faced with a task or challenge we must resolve, we are most open to acquiring the knowledge and skills required to respond. This is the motivational power of Immersive learning designs in which a problem or task assignment initiates and drives learning.

by Ann Kwinn & C. Kwinn

In this chapter we will apply proven guidelines to learning environments that use an immersive architecture. Specifically we will review 1) the features and components of immersive training, 2) what can go wrong, and 3) evidence on the use of media to present immersive case scenarios.

The Power of Immersion

We saw in chapter 4 that immersive learning environments (also called whole-task, scenario-based, or problem-based learning) can accelerate expertise simply by compressing experience. By resolving realistic work situations in a short time frame, experience that could take months on the job can be squeezed into a few training days. Compressed experience is especially useful in settings where it could take years to acquire certain types of expertise. Some examples include all forms of diagnostic tasks faced by health professionals, sales professionals, or service technicians as well as design tasks that require critical and creative thinking such as design of a website or project plan. On the job it could take years to troubleshoot specific failures which can be simulated in immersive lesson designs. In fact, Gott & Lesgold (2000) found that 25 hours of practice on an immersive computer-based troubleshooting simulation accelerated the expertise of two-year Air Force technicians to the equivalent of ten-year veterans! When job performance relies on critical thinking skills, immersive lessons can teach those skills in the context of problem solving. In other words, they can teach not only what to do but the reasoning behind the decisions and actions taken.

Immersive lessons are motivating to many learners. By starting a learning event with a real-world task assignment, the relevance of the training is immediately salient. Problems with an optimal level of challenge and guidance have the potential to increase learner engagement leading to deeper processing and better learning.

A third benefit is transfer of learning. Because all learning occurs in the context of real-world types of tasks and problems, the cues accumulated in long-term memory will lead to better retrieval later. When facing a new problem on the job, most experts search their memory banks for a similar situation they faced in the past. Problem-based lessons give learners an opportunity to build those memory repositories for later use.

Immersive designs are most appropriate when teaching learners such as apprentices with some relevant experience how to perform tasks that rely on critical and creative problem solving. They are especially useful to teach skills that are difficult to acquire on the job because of safety concerns or scarcity of real-world opportunities. Teaching new military officers to make good combat decisions is one example. Decisions can have life or death consequences and an immersive approach to learning offers at least a partial substitute for real-world experience.

What Do You Think?

Place a check next to each statement you believe is true:

- ☐ A. Immersive learning environments require computer simulations.
- ☐ B. Immersive lessons are more expensive to develop than stair-step lessons.
- ☐ C. Immersive lessons should include feedback.
- ☐ D. Learning in immersive lessons is better when realistic multimedia such as video is used to present scenarios.
- ☐ E. Immersive lessons can be delivered in a classroom or asynchronous multimedia environment.

The Anatomy of an Immersive Lesson

There are four essential elements of an effective immersive lesson: 1) an authentic problem or task assignment that serves as a context for learning, 2) guidance in solving the problem, 3) feedback on problem solutions or problem-solving processes, and 4) explicit opportunities to reflect on problem solutions.

I'll describe each of these in a bit more detail and illustrate with the Excel content used in chapter 12 as well as with a multimedia automotive troubleshooting lesson produced by Raytheon Professional Services.

1. The Problem

Case study scenarios commonly appear in stair-step lessons and sometimes even in show-and-tell lessons. In stair-step lessons the problem or case study serves as an end-of-lesson (or end-of-unit) practice opportunity. But in the immersive approach, the lesson starts (rather than ends) with a problem that serves as the context for learning. You can see two examples in figures 13.1 and 13.2. Figure 13.1 shows the case that initiates an Excel classroom lesson with some business analysis goals for Pete's Pet Emporium. The screen capture in figure 13.2 shows the work order for troubleshooting an automotive failure in a virtual shop.

Figure 13.1. An Excel Assignment Initiates and Drives an Immersive Lesson

Excel Case 1: Pete's Pet Emporium

Pete has always done his bookkeeping manually and is looking to you for help as he converts to an online spreadsheet. Your first task is to show Pete the value of using formulas in his spreadsheet. For Pete's first lesson, you plan to show him how to use a formula to calculate total costs, sales and net gain for January.

	A	B	C	D	E	F
1						
2			Pete's Pet Emporium			
3			January			
4		Products	Cost	Sales	Net	% Sales
5						
6		Grooming	$5,000	$12,000		
7						
8		Feed	$10,000	$25,000		
9						
10		Toys	$3,000	$5,000		
11						
12		Accessory	$5,000	$8,000		
13						
14		Misc	$2,000	$7,000		
15						
16		TOTAL				
17						
18						
19						

Designing an effective problem or scenario is one of your biggest challenges. First, your problem must incorporate the key skills needed to resolve it. In the Excel class, the business analyst will require the use of formulas to perform calculations and charts to display data. In the troubleshooting lesson, the technician will need to learn the mechanical and electrical components of the systems involved, which diagnostic tests might be most appropriate, and how to interpret diagnostic data to identify a likely cause of failure.

 As you plan your problem, define the desired outcome and the criteria for success. These elements correspond to the action and criterion

Figure 13.2. A Work Order Kicks Off an Automotive Troubleshooting Lesson

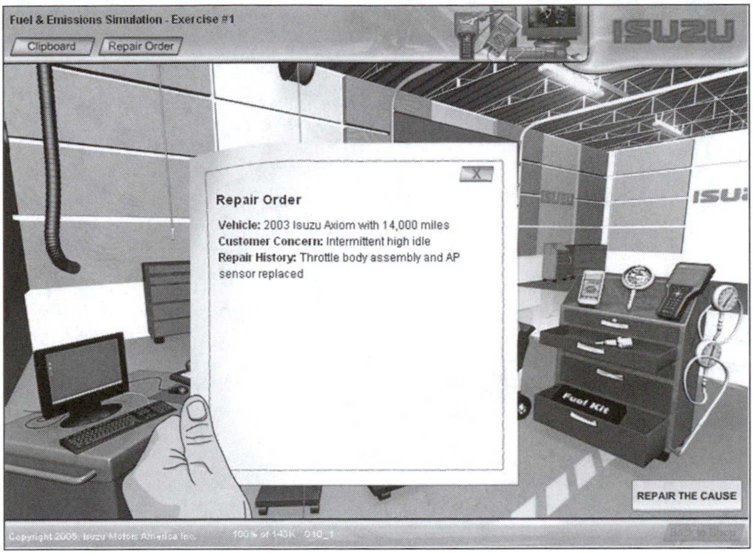

With permission from Raytheon Professional Services.

of a traditional lesson objective. Your outcome may involve a decision, actions, rationale for actions, a problem-solving path, or a product. Your criteria may be a correct answer, an answer that matches rationale, a decision path that is efficient and effective, solution time, or specified features of a product deliverable to name a few. For example, the Excel class will initially require the construction and input of accurate formulas to achieve the assigned goals. The outcome will be a correct answer since the spreadsheet incorporates specific data values. In contrast, the automotive troubleshooting class will require 1) selection of a correct diagnosis, as well as 2) application of a time efficient logical problem-solving process in which irrelevant tests are not conducted.

Many problems will require the learner to access-related problem data. For example, in figure 13.3, you can see a simulated automatic shop offering the technician access to a variety of common diagnostic tools and tests. This part of your design will correspond to the "givens" in your learning

Figure 13.3. A Virtual Repair Shop Includes Normal Testing Tools

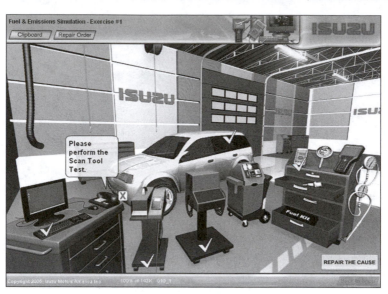

With permission from Raytheon Professional Services.

objective. When you do your job analysis, note the common sources of data that experts use to solve problems and incorporate them into your lesson. Typical examples might be documents, technical diagrams, computer programs, client interviews, test equipment—any resources that would be normally used on the job to gather data about the problem.

2. The Guidance

One of the potential minefields in immersive learning is mental overload and learner confusion leading to frustration and drop out. Give a lot of thought to the type and placement of guidance in the scenarios. Instructional psychologists call this type of guidance *scaffolding*. For the initial problems in your immersive environment, provide a lot of guidance and gradually remove the level of support as learning progresses. The most common types of guidance that I'll review include: 1) problem sequencing, 2) learner control, 3) demonstrations, and 4) knowledge resources such as experts, stair-step tutorials, and/or references.

Sequence Problems from Easy to Hard. The initial problem or task assignment should be the simplest instance you can develop of an authentic job problem. Easy problems will have fewer variables, relaxed constraints, straightforward solutions, and limited amounts of data to consider. The first Excel problem might require a column addition or row subtraction. A later problem might require several operations such as subtraction and division. For automotive troubleshooting, initial cases could involve a single system (such as electrical with a straightforward failure).

Constrain Learner Control. Learner options are limited in a more structured immersive design called a *branched scenario*. Figure 13.4 shows a screen shot from a customer service branched scenario lesson. The learner hears the customer's comments and has a choice of three response options. Upon clicking any of the options, the learner sees and hears the customer response and receives commentary from the virtual coach in the lower left corner. These types of immersive designs are especially effective for problems in which one choice leads to another and then another in a linear timeline sequence.

Figure 13.4. A Branched Scenario Immersive Lesson on Customer Service

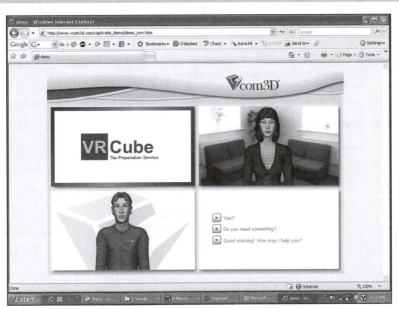

With permission from Vcom3D.

227

You can design immersive training to offer higher or lower degrees of freedom for learners to access program elements. The automotive troubleshooting design could allow a lot of freedom if learners can access any of the testing tools in any sequence they wish. In early problem solving, though, you may want to "disable" some of the interface to help learners stay on track. Clicking on irrelevant test equipment will simply lead to an onscreen message that this test is not relevant to the current situation. Later problem assignments can offer all of the testing options.

Alternate Problem Demonstrations with Assignments. Start with a demonstration of how to solve a problem. For example, the instructor might demonstrate how to add a column of numbers in the spreadsheet. Next ask learners to perform a similar task using different data. For example, the learners would add or subtract a different column or row. A more sophisticated technique is to start with a full demonstration and then move to a partial demonstration in which the instruction completes the first solution steps and the learner finishes it. End with a full problem assignment that the learner solves on their own.

Offer Knowledge Resources: Experts, Peer Collaboration, Tutorials, and References. Some problems can benefit from a variety of perspectives. For example, a medical ethics problem provides links to virtual experts including lawyer, ethicist, clergy, psychologist, and colleague. A course for new supervisors offers links to manager, experienced supervisor, legal staff, and human resources (HR), to name a few. The automotive troubleshooting course includes a telephone that offers advice about which tests to try. In addition, learners can work on problems collaboratively. Discussion of alternatives in a group setting encourages deeper processing of information. Working with a partner in a virtual world immersive science lesson led to better problem-solving learning than working alone (Barab et al. 2009).

In situations that involve unfamiliar procedural knowledge, a virtual manual could offer access to a stair-step tutorial. The tutorial might teach a procedure or explain company policy, for example. An onscreen computer or manual might open to actual company references. An automotive repair lesson might include a computer that links to the company online help system.

3. The Feedback

All learning benefits from feedback. In immersive learning environments you can use two types of feedback: intrinsic and instructive. *Instructive feedback* is traditional feedback that tells the learners that they are correct or incorrect and provides an explanation. The virtual coach in lower left of figure 13.4 offers this type of feedback. *Intrinsic feedback* shows the outcomes of learners' actions or decisions as they resolve the problem. In other words, the learner takes actions and sees how the situation plays out for better or for worse. For example, in figure 13.4, when the learner selects a rude comment, the customer responds negatively. In the automotive repair scenario, selecting an incorrect diagnosis leads to a screen showing the original problem is unresolved.

Intrinsic feedback can also reveal environmental responses that may be normally hidden. For example, a food handlers lesson scenario incorporated a germ meter that reached the danger zone when food was improperly touched. A supervisory lesson on giving performance feedback included a motivation dial to reveal the feelings of the employee receiving feedback.

4. The Reflection

One of the big differences between immersive and stair-step lessons is the instructional attitude toward learner errors. Based on behaviorist roots, stair-step courses attempt to minimize learner errors. When a mistake is made, the learner usually gets immediate corrective feedback. In contrast, immersive course designs see mistakes as an opportunity for learning. Feedback may not come until several actions have been taken or even at the end of the scenario. To learn from mistakes, it's critical to reflect on what you did and alternative actions you might take. One powerful form of feedback that encourages reflection is an expert comparison. In figure 13.5, I show a screen from the automotive troubleshooting lesson that displays side by side the diagnostic actions taken and time consumed by the learner and by an expert. Another approach is to let the learner experience intrinsic feedback and give them an opportunity to reconsider and replay their choices.

What Can Go Wrong with Immersive Lessons?

There are a number of potential traps to avoid in immersive lessons.

Learner Overload

Perhaps the most common problem encountered in immersive lessons is mental overload. Asking a learner to solve a problem unfamiliar to them and to learn the knowledge and skills they need to resolve that problem at the same time can be overwhelming. That's why immersive approaches are generally not advised for novice learners. It's also the reason that the guidance elements I discussed at the beginning of this chapter are so critical for success.

Figure 13.5. A Learner Can Compare Their Solution Process with that of an Expert

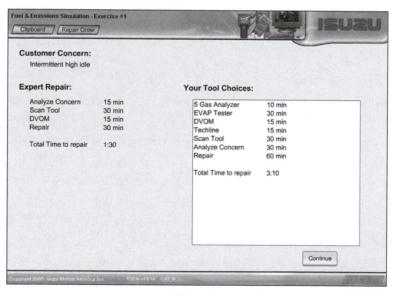

With permission from Raytheon Professional Services.

Unbalanced Skill Set

So far I've focused primarily on the elements of a single immersive lesson. Imagine, however, in medical education that all of your case problems focus on a broken leg. Clearly, the range of knowledge and skills acquired would be very limited. To achieve balance, you need to identify "problem classes" based on the diversity of work-role functions you identify during your job analysis. For example, you might have scenarios that focus on different types of heart failure, oncology, orthopedic issues, and so on. Within each problem class, you will need to identify a series of problems that incorporate the required knowledge and skills of that class and that progress from easy to complex.

Inefficiency

Inefficiency is an offspring of high "flounder-factor" lessons. When learners start to take random actions to progress through a problem, the result can be both ineffective and inefficient learning. Learner control is one of the major tools you can use to minimize inefficiency. As I mentioned under our discussion of guidance, you can present more constrained interfaces (branched scenarios, limited active objects) to direct learners during early problem-solving stages and also be more aggressive with imposing guidance and directions when learners get off track.

Instructor Roles

In the classroom it is up to the instructor to administer and facilitate the case problems. Specifically, the instructor can present the problem, provide relevant clarifications, facilitate group discussions, help locate relevant resources, and mediate problem debriefs. Note that these activities are quite different from a more traditional role. Instructors must switch from the "sage on the stage" to the "guide on the side." The degree of ambiguity in the process and in the final results may be difficult for some instructors to accept—especially if they are used to working in highly directive stair-step environments or in instructor-centered show-and-tell environments.

Media in Immersive Learning Environments

Is it better to present a problem scenario in text or with richer forms of media such as video or computer animation? We have some preliminary data suggesting that often learners will become more engaged when the scenario is presented with visuals rather than text. My colleagues at Microsoft taught an instructor-led security networking course for years using a case study presented primarily in text. The case study used a fictitious pharmaceutical company. The instructors converted the text case into a multimedia format by creating a mock website for the case company and adding video interviews and online networking diagrams. The instructors reported that the learners were much more engaged with the multimedia version and treated the scenario more like an actual client engagement.

There is some research evidence that supports this anecdotal observation. For example, Kamin and her colleagues (2003) compared collaborative discussions among medical students who reviewed a case in text with discussions among medical students who reviewed the same case in video. The discussions were much richer in groups using the video case. Of course, in medicine the sights and sounds of the patient can be presented in a much more authentic manner in video than in text. Finally, Moreno and Ortegano-Layne (2008) compared learner ratings and learning among student teachers provided case examples presented in text, computer animation, or video. Both ratings and learning were better from the computer-animated and video cases than from the text cases. The computer-animated and video cases resulted in nearly equivalent learning and ratings.

Based on the limited data we have, I recommend adding visual elements to a problem scenario whether it will be conducted in a classroom or computer setting. Realistic media is likely to be especially helpful to portray case elements that involve sights and sounds not as authentically represented in text. It also can create a more compelling environment that engages learners more deeply.

The Bottom Line

What Do You Think?

Now that you have reviewed the evidence, here are my comments:

☐ A. Immersive lessons require computer simulations.

FALSE. Immersive lessons do not require computer simulations. Some can be done with simple branching. More complex forms do involve some level of simulation.

☐ B. Immersive lessons are more expensive to develop than stair-step lessons.

OFTEN TRUE. Of course many factors affect development costs including the media used, the incorporation of simulations, complexity of the case problems, and others. Stair-step architectures are generally more straight forward to design because they require decisions regarding segmenting and sequencing of content and insertion of frequent application-level practice. In contrast, immersive designs tend to take a more holistic approach and may require more upfront design time. However, after completing one or two immersive lessons, a template can be adapted to accommodate new case variables and data. Also, some authoring systems include a programming interface for branched-scenario designs.

☐ C. Immersive lessons should include feedback.

TRUE. In addition to traditional instructional feedback, you can add the opportunity for the learner to play out the scenario and see the consequences of her decisions. This type of feedback should be linked to reflection to ensure learners take time to review their actions and consider action alternatives.

☐ D. Learning in immersive lessons is better when realistic multimedia such as video is included.

TRUE. We need more evidence on this question, but the few studies to date indicate that a more visual presentation of a case scenario can be more compelling than a text presentation.

☐ E. Immersive lessons can be delivered in a classroom or asynchronous multimedia environment.

TRUE. A multimedia case could be designed for debrief in a classroom setting or could be self-contained for individual or partner self-study.

Quality Assurance Checklist

☐ The immersive approach is used for tasks that involve decision making and critical and creative thinking as well as for learners with some relevant background.

☐ Lessons kick off with a work-authentic assignment or scenario.

☐ The interface is clean, and learner response options are clear.

☐ Initial scenarios incorporate fewer variables and less data than later problems.

☐ Initial scenarios offer less learner control than later problems.

☐ Multiple forms of guidance minimize learner frustration and ensure learning.

☐ Guidance is faded as learners gain more experience.

☐ Both intrinsic and instructional feedback are provided.

☐ Feedback can show both visible and "invisible" consequences of actions.

☐ Learners have the opportunity to make mistakes, experience the results, and reflect to learn from their mistakes.

☐ Scenarios are presented with visuals rather than with text alone.

☐ Instructors assume the role of a facilitator rather than a director or knowledge source.

☐ Multiple cases incorporate the full range of knowledge and skills to fulfill the goals of the instructional program.

For More Information

Clark, R.C. (2009). "Accelerating expertise with scenario-based learning." *T+D* (January): 84–5.

Clark, R.C. (2008). *Building Expertise*, 3d ed. San Francisco: Pfeiffer. See ch. 13.

Part V

What's Next?

In this final chapter I revisit the four myths described in chapter 1 with a look to the future of evidence-based workforce learning.

♦ ♦ ♦

Beyond Training Fads and Fiction

♦ ♦ ♦

Chapter 14

Beyond Training Fads and Fiction

"Unlike medicine, agriculture, and industrial production, the field of education operates largely on the basis of ideology and professional consensus. As such, it is subject to fads and is incapable of the cumulative progress that follows from the application of the scientific method. . . . We will change education to make it an evidence-based field." —U.S. Department of Education (2002), 48

In the future, training decisions may be based more on evidence than fiction.

TRAINING FUTURES

I had it good for a while there.

by Ann Kwinn & C. Kwinn

In spite of a commitment to evidence-based education, progress has been slow. I believe training practitioners in private workforce learning enterprises are better positioned to leverage research than our colleagues in the public education sector.

Throughout this book, we've reviewed evidence and psychology for training techniques you can use to optimize learning. In this final chapter, I want to summarize our journey and suggest that workforce learning professionals like you can be the groundbreakers in bridging the gap between research and practice.

Blood, Phlegm, Black and Yellow Bile

We started in chapter 1 by considering that just about 400 years ago common wisdom held that blood was produced by the heart and the liver and was continuously used up by the body. In other words, there was no accurate conception of blood circulation. We've come a long way since the emergence of the scientific method in the seventeenth century. Just as other applied fields— initially the health sciences and more recently psychology—have formally embraced evidence-based practice, the time has come for training practitioners to professionalize.

The time is right because it is only now in the early twenty-first century that we are accumulating a sufficient body of related evidence to inform our instructional decisions. Of course, we have a long way to go and much more evidence to seek. Still, it's time. We have enough evidence and know enough about the psychology of learning to make sound recommendations to our clients. Imagine that evidence-based practice were to really put down roots in the training field. What differences would we see?

What Do You Think?

Put a check next to each statement that you think is an accurate prediction for workforce learning over the next five years:

- ☐ A. You will see and hear less about learning styles.
- ☐ B. New technologies will be exploited for training in ways that accommodate the strengths and limits of the human brain.
- ☐ C. Courses, as we know them today, will die.
- ☐ D. Universal training panaceas will be eschewed in favor of tactics tailored for specific outcomes and audiences.
- ☐ E. Training practitioners will integrate evidence, psychology, experience, and organizational culture and constraints as they plan, develop, and deliver learning environments.

In chapter 1 we reviewed four prevalent training myths. In this final chapter, I'll revisit those myths through a lens of evidence-based practice.

Training Myth 1: Learning Styles

I believe that like the four body humors of blood, phlegm, black and yellow bile, we're overdue to retire the learning styles myths in favor of more valid individual differences among our learners. We've reviewed ample evidence showing that when learning something new, we are all visual learners—that is, all novices benefit from a relevant visual added to words. We've also seen that we are all auditory learners. Evidence shows that when viewing a complex visual such as an animation, we all benefit from an audio explanation rather than a detailed text explanation.

Rather than learning styles, what individual differences should we consider? Prior knowledge is the most important. Recall from chapter 5 that visuals promote learning for individuals new to the topic but do little for those with more experience. Because learners with related prior knowledge have mental models in long-term memory, they do not need the same kind or level of training support as novices. For example, an apprentice can benefit from an immersive lesson design, whereas most novices need the more defined structure of the stair-step approach.

Rather than investing resources in learning styles, consider some form of adaptive instruction in which you assess the prior knowledge of your learners and prescribe lessons that tailor instruction—not only the content but also the instructional tactics. For example, a learning management system will route the novice learner to more directive lessons while offering learners with relevant background more open learning environments. The system may even track emerging expertise of a learner and dynamically adjust training methods to evolving needs. If your organization includes a heterogeneous population, an investment in adaptive learning can pay off in better and more efficient learning.

My hope is that the training community will redirect the resources currently invested in learning styles to evidence-based techniques per my guideline from chapter 1.

◆ ◆ ◆

Fads & Fiction Guideline 1:

Do not waste your training resources on learning styles, including instructor training, measurement of learning styles, or training methods that attempt to accommodate learning styles.

◆ ◆ ◆

Training Myth 2: Media Panaceas

Although new media are always engaging, we have ample evidence that learning effectiveness relies on the use of instructional tactics that support the human brain. Therefore as we embrace new media for training, the professional trainer will consider how the various features of those media can be leveraged in ways that support learning. She will keep in mind the limits of working memory. She will manage mental load through a judicious use of visuals, audio, and text. She will find ways to help learners build new knowledge through productive media engagement.

The Death of the Course and Learning 2.0

From smart mobile devices to virtual classrooms to social media, new technology may spell the end of courses as we have known them for the past 100 years. Will courses per se die? Probably not. However, we can align our various technologies to construct a dynamic performance platform that weaves together formal and informal learning venues, job task feedback, and performance support, to name a few. The result is formal support for learning that is ongoing and occurs in the workplace context as well as the classroom. Increasingly teaching and learning become the shared responsibility of everyone in the enterprise.

As this more pervasive learning environment emerges, we will abandon a technology-centric view for a learner-centered perspective.

Fads & Fiction Guideline 2:

Ignore panaceas in the guise of technology solutions in favor of leveraging an array of media to transition from a focus on isolated training events to a continuum of pervasive learning and teaching opportunities.

◆ ◆ ◆

Training Myth 3: The More They Like It, the More They Learn

No doubt we will continue to collect student ratings of our learning events. And the 2.0 web will offer many more avenues for the community to discuss and improve learning events. We've seen evidence that there is little linkage between course ratings and learning from that course. Still, our learners are one of our primary customers. Therefore, I hope we will broaden our collection of learner reactions and use that data judiciously. Research points the way to survey questions that are more productive than many used today. For example, Sitzmann et al. (2008) found that posttraining self-reported ratings of confidence are the most useful predictor of learning outcomes. To measure self-efficacy incorporate questions such as "rate your level of confidence to apply the workshop skills to your job."

I hope the training community will supplement end-of-course student ratings with additional evidence of learning and application of learning in the workplace. This can be in the form of tests, projects, blogs, wikis, and the diverse new social media applications to come, as well as metrics related to enterprise goals such as safety incidents, productivity, customer satisfaction, and others. Yes, these measures will require additional time. However, many are collected already. And when systematically reviewed, they can give us a much more comprehensive picture of the benefits of a broad enterprise learning environment on organizational objectives.

◆ ◆ ◆

Fads & Fiction Guideline 3:

Don't rely on course satisfaction surveys as sole indicators of learning. Use valid tests to assess the pedagogical effectiveness of any learning environment as well as performance improvement metrics.

◆ ◆ ◆

Training Myth 4: Stories (Games or You-Name-It) Promote Learning

From engineering to computer programming, all applied domains are subject to the latest fads. It's human nature to gravitate to the shiny penny! And in most cases, training innovations hit the practitioners' world ahead of research results. So you will often need to initially evaluate the latest trends in the absence of evidence. However, keep in mind that there are very few instructional techniques that are universally effective. In most cases you need to evaluate claims by asking:

1. What are the core features of the latest cool trend?

2. For whom would this technique or technology be most appropriate?

3. For what kinds of learning goals does it best apply?

4. How does this new trend support the limits and strengths of our human memory systems?

5. How can I best adapt the new practice to the culture, staff, and constraints of my organization?

Don't forget the "No Yellow Brick Road Effect": There are few best practices that will work for all learners and for all learning goals. The evidence that has accumulated over years of research on general categories like graphics and games is the basis for my fourth recommendation.

◆ ◆ ◆

Fads & Fiction Guideline 4:

Be skeptical about claims for the universal effectiveness of any instructional technique. Always ask: How is the technique defined? For whom is it useful? For what kinds of learning outcomes does it work?

◆ ◆ ◆

What's Next?

Research on best methods to use in workforce learning is just in its infancy. Even so, I believe that those of us in workforce learning are better positioned to embrace evidence-based practice than our colleagues in public education. School systems in the United States face enormous challenges, many of which are more muted in our worlds. For example, a policy of universal public education leads to a population of very heterogenous learners. School systems are local entities subject to diverse and changing value systems and political pressures. As a result, systemic change processes across a district, a state, or a nation are rare. In contrast, workforce learning aims for the cost-effective realization of operational goals by a preselected staff. Learning environments and techniques that are proven to be more effective face fewer hurdles compared to the public education sector.

Big gaps remain between research and practice. My hope is that funding for applied educational research—which is now inconsistent and miniscule compared to other applied fields such as medicine and engineering—will grow. Additionally, we need processes to find, synthesize, and translate evidence that currently appears among diverse scholarly journals. Today is it almost impossible for a busy workforce learning practitioner to amass and synthesize research findings.

Perhaps in a not too distant future we will see increased collaboration between the research community and workforce learning organizations to build conduits for the conduct and dissemination of educational research.

Many latent opportunities hide within our professional organizations, publishers, for-profit training providers, universities, and corporations.

The Bottom Line

Let's conclude by revisiting the questions you considered at the start of the chapter.

What Do You Think?

Put a check next to each statement that you think is an accurate prediction for workforce learning over the next five years:

- ☐ A. You will see and hear less about learning styles.
- ☐ B. New technologies will be exploited for training in ways that accommodate the strengths and limits of the human brain.
- ☐ C. Courses, as we know them today, will die.
- ☐ D. Universal training panaceas will be eschewed in favor of tactics tailored for specific outcomes and audiences.
- ☐ E. Training practitioners will become critical thinkers who integrate evidence, psychology, experience, and organizational culture and constraints as they plan, develop, and deliver learning environments.

OK—on this final exercise—I leave the answers to you because in fact the real answers will depend on how practitioners like you and professional associations like ASTD (American Society for Training & Development), APA (American Psychological Association), and AERA (American Educational Research Association) decide to sponsor, identify, communicate, and apply evidence that guides daily practice.

I hope this book is one step along the way.

For More Information

Burkhardt, H., & A.H. Schoenfeld (2003). "Improving educational research: Toward a more useful, more influential, and better-funded enterprise." *Educational Researcher, 32,* 3–14.

References

APA Presidential Task Force on Evidence-Based Practice. (2006). Evidence-based practice in psychology. *American Psychologist* 61, 271–85.

Atkinson, R.K., A. Renkl, & M.M. Merrill. (2003). Transitioning from studying examples to solving problems: Effects of self-explanation prompts and fading worked out steps. *Journal of Educational Psychology* 95(4): 774–83.

Ayres, P., N. Marcus, C. Chan, & N. Qian. (2009). Learning hand manipulative tasks: When instructional animations are superior to equivalent static representations. *Computers in Human Behavior* 25, 348–53.

Barab, S.A., B. Scott, S. Siyahhan, R. Goldstone, A. Ingram-Globe, S.J. Zuiker, & S. Warren. (2009). Transformation play as a curricular scaffold: Using video games to support science education. *Journal Science Educational Technology* 18, 305–20.

Bernard, R.M., P.C. Abrami, Y. Lou, E. Borokhovski, A. Wade, L. Wozney, P.A. Wallet, M. Fisher, & B. Huang. (2004). How does distance education compare with classroom instruction? A meta-analysis of the empirical literature. *Review of Educational Research* 74, 379–439.

Bligh, D.A. (2000). *What's the Use of Lectures?* San Francisco: Jossey-Bass.

Brewer, N., S. Harey, & C. Semmler. (2004). Improving comprehension of jury instructions with audio-visual presentation. *Applied Cognitive Psychology* 18, 765–76.

Burkhardt, H., & A.H. Schoenfeld. (2003). Improving educational research: Toward a more useful, more influential, and better-funded enterprise. *Educational Researcher* 32, 3–14.

Butcher, K.R. (2006). Learning from text with diagrams: Promoting mental model development and inference generation. *Journal of Educational Psychology* 98(1): 182–97.

Chi, M.T.H. (2000). Self-explaining expository texts: The dual processes of generating inferences and repairing mental models. In *Advances in instructional psychology: Educational design and cognitive science*, ed. R. Glaser. Mahwah, NJ: Lawrence Erlbaum Associates.

Clark, R.C. (2009). Accelerating expertise with scenario-based learning. *T+D* (January): 84–5.

———. (2008). *Building Expertise*, 3d ed. San Francisco: Pfeiffer.

———. (2008). *Developing Technical Training*, 3d ed. San Francisco: Pfeiffer.

Clark, R.C., & A. Kwinn. (2007). *The New Virtual Classroom*. San Francisco: Pfeiffer.

Clark, R.C., & C. Lyons. (in press). *Graphics for Learning*, 2d ed. San Francisco: Pfeiffer.

Clark, R.C., & R.E. Mayer, (2008a). Learning by viewing versus learning by doing: Evidence-based guidelines for principled learning environments. *Performance Improvement* 47, 5–13.

——— (2008b). *e-Learning & the Science of Instruction*, 2d ed. San Francisco: Pfeiffer.

Cook, D.A., W.G. Thompson, K.G. Thomas, & M.R. Thomas. (2009). Lack of interaction between sensing-intuitive learning styles and problem-first versus information-first instruction: A randomized crossover trial. *Advances in Health Science Education* 14, 70–90.

Ericcson, K.A. (2006). The influence of experience and deliberate practice on the development of superior expert performance. In *The Cambridge Handbook of Expertise and Expert Performance*, ed. K.A. Ericsson, N. Charness, P.J. Feltovich, & R.R. Hoffman. New York: Cambridge University Press.

Gick, M.L., & K.J. Holyoak. (1980). Analogical problem solving. *Cognitive Psychology* 12, 306–55.

Ginns, P. (2005). Integrating information: A meta-analysis of spatial contiguity and temporal contiguity effects. *Learning and Instruction* 16, 511–25.

Gott, S.P., & A.M. Lesgold. (2000). Competence in the workplace: How cognitive performance models and situated instruction can accelerate skill acquisition. In *Advances in Instructional Psychology: Educational Design and Cognitive Science,* ed. R. Glaser. Mahwah, NJ: Lawrence Erlbaum Associates.

Haidet, P., R.O. Morgan, K. O'Malley, B.J. Moran, & B.F. Richards. (2004). A controlled trial of active versus passive learning strategies in a large group setting. *Advances in Health Sciences Education* 9, 15–27.

Hatala, R.M., L.R. Brooks, & G.R. Normal. (2003). Practice makes perfect: The critical role of mixed practice in the acquisition of ECG interpretation skills. *Advances in Health Sciences Education* 8, 17–26.

Kalyuga, S., P. Chandler, J. Tuovinen, & J. Sweller. (2001). When problem solving is superior to studying worked examples. *Journal of Educational Psychology* 93, 579–88.

Kamin, C.S., P.S. O'Sullivan, R. Deterding, & M. Younger. (2003). A comparison of critical thinking in groups of third-year medical students in text, video, and virtual PBL case modalities. *Academic Medicine* 78(2): 204–11.

Kratzig, G.P., & K.D. Arbuthnott. (2006). Perceptual learning style and learning proficiency: A test of the hypothesis. *Journal of Educational Psychology* 98, 238–46.

Krause, U., R. Stark, & H. Mandl. (2009). The effects of cooperative learning and feedback on e-learning in statistics. *Learning and Instruction* 19, 158–70.

Kumta, S.M., P.L. Tsang, L.K. Hung, & J.C.Y. Cheng. (2003). Fostering critical thinking skills through a web-based tutorial programme for final-year medical students: A randomized controlled study. *Journal of Educational Multimedia and Hypermedia* 12, 267–73.

Levasseru, D.G., & J.K. Sawyer. (2006). Pedagogy meets PowerPoint: A research review of the effects of computer-generated slides in the classroom. *The Review of Communication* 6, 101–23.

Lim, J., R.A. Reiser, & Z. Olina. (2009). The effects of part-task and whole-task instructional approaches on acquisition and transfer of a complex cognitive skill. *Educational Technology Research & Development* 57, 61–77.

Lusk, M.M., & R.K. Atkinson. (2007). Animated pedagogical agents: Does the degree of embodiment impact learning from static or animated worked examples? *Applied Cognitive Psychology* 21, 747–64.

Marsh, E.J., & H.E. Sink. (2009). Access to handouts of presentation slides during lecture: consequences for learning. *Applied Cognitive Psychology*. In press.

Mayer, R.E. (2009). *Multimedia Learning*, 2d ed. New York: Cambridge University Press.

Mayer, R.E., A. Bove, A. Bryman, R. Mars, & L. Tapangco. (1996). When less is more: Meaningful learning from visual and verbal summaries of science textbook lessons. *Journal of Educational Psychology* 88, 64–73.

Mayer, R.E., M. Hegarty, S. Mayer, & J. Campbell. (2005). When static media promote active learning: Annotated illustrations versus narrated animations in multimedia learning. *Journal of Experimental Psychology: Applied* 11, 256–65.

Mayer, R.E., & C.I. Johnson. (2008). Revising the redundancy principle in multimedia learning. *Journal of Educational Psychology* 100, 380–6.

Mayer, R.E., A. Mathias, & K. Wetzell. (2002). Fostering understanding of multimedia messages through pretraining: Evidence for a two-stage theory of mental model construction. *Journal of Experimental Psychology: Applied* 8, 147–54.

Mayer, R.E., & R. Moreno. (1998). A split-attention effect in multimedia learning: Evidence for dual processing systems in working memory. *Journal of Educational Psychology* 90, 312–20.

Mayer, R.E., V. Sims, & H. Tajika. (1995). A comparison of how textbooks teach mathematical problem solving in Japan and the United States. *American Educational Research Journal* 32, 443–60.

Mayer, R.E., A. Stull, K. DeLeeuw, K. Almeroth, B. Bimber, D. Chun, M. Bulger, J. Campbell, A. Knight, & H. Zhang. (2009). Clickers in college classrooms: Fostering learning with questioning methods in large lecture classes. *Contemporary Educational Psychology* 34, 51–7.

Moreno, R. (2006). Does the modality principle hold for different media? A test of the methods-affects-learning hypothesis. *Journal of Computer Assisted Learning* 33, 149–58.

————. (2004). Decreasing cognitive load for novice students: Effects of explanatory versus corrective feedback in discovery-based multimedia. *Instructional Science* 32, 99–113.

Moreno, R., & R.E. Mayer. (2000). A coherence effect in multimedia learning: The case for minimizing irrelevant sounds in the design of multimedia messages. *Journal of Educational Psychology* 92, 117–25.

Moreno, R., & L. Ortegano-Layne. (2008). Do classroom exemplars promote the application of principles in teacher education? A comparison of videos, animations, and narratives. *Educational Technology Research & Development* 56, 449–65.

Nielsen Report (2009). Global faces and networked places: A Nielsen report on social networking's new global footprint.

Paradise, A. (2009). *ASTD 2009 State of Industry Report*. Alexandria, VA: ASTD.

Paradi, D. (2005). Are we wasting $250 million per day due to bad Point-Point? Downloaded July 2009 from http://www.thinkoutsidetheslide. com/articles/wasting_250M_bad_ppt.htm.

Rohrer, E., & K. Taylor. (2007). The shuffling of mathematics problems improves learning. *Instructional Science* 35, 481–98.

————. (2006). The effects of overlearning and distributed practice on the retention of mathematics knowledge. *Applied Cognitive Psychology* 20, 1209–24.

Sackett,, D.L., W.M. Rosenberg, J.A. Gray, R.B. Haynes, & W.S. Richardson. (1996). Evidence-based medicine: What it is and what it isn't. *British Medical Journal* 312, 71–2.

Schwan, S., & R. Riempp. (2004). The cognitive benefits of interactive videos: Learning to tie nautical knots. *Learning & Instruction* 14, 293–305.

Sitzmann, T., K.G. Brown, W.J. Casper, K. Ely, & R.D. Zimmerman. (2008). A review and meta-analysis of the nomological network of trainee reactions. *Journal of Appplied Psychology* 93, 280–295.

Strayer, D.L., D. Crouch, & F.A. Drews. (2006). A comparison of the cell-phone driver and the drunk driver. *Human Factors* 46, 640–9.

Sweller, J., & G.A. Cooper. (1985). The use of worked examples as a substitute for problem solving in learning algebra. *Cognition and Instruction* 2, 59–89.

U.S. Department of Education. (2002). Strategic plan for 2002–2007. Cited in Burkhardt & Schoenfeld (2003).

Wang, N., W.L. Johnson, R.E. Mayer, P. Rizzo, E. Shaw, & H. Collins. (2008). The politeness effect: Pedagogical agents and learning outcomes. *International Journal of Human Computer Studies* 66, 96–112.

Glossary

Agent   See Learning Agent.

Application Practice   Assignments that ask learners to respond in ways they would respond on the job. Contrast with recall practice.

Architecture   See Instructional Architecture.

Asynchronous e-learning   Computer learning environments in which individual learners study independently at their own pace usually in a self-study mode.

Attention   The allocation of limited working memory capacity to specific internal or external information.

Automaticity   Any task that is hardwired into long-term memory can be performed without using working memory resources. Automaticity is built through repetition.

Behavioral Engagement   Overt activity in the service of learning.

Behaviorist   A psychological theory that emphasizes the role of stimulus-response in human learning and behavior. Popular during the mid-1900s.

Blocked Practice   An organizational scheme in which practice addressing a specific skill is grouped together. Contrast with Mixed Practice.

Branched Scenario   A specific form of immersive training in which learners respond to a limited number of choices as they progress through the e-learning lesson.

Coherence Effect   Disruption of learning from lesson additions that are irrelevant to the learning goal such as stories or visuals added for interest.

Collaborative Learning   Instructional technique in which two or more learners work together to achieve a learning goal.

Cognitive Overload   A condition stemming from exceeding the limited capacity of working memory. When overloaded, working memory processing becomes inefficient. Also called mental load.

Concept   A type of knowledge in which a single term refers to multiple specific instances. Computer and lesson are two examples.

Declarative Knowledge   Concepts and facts stored in memory that are easy to articulate. The names of equipment parts and a description of how equipment works are two examples.

Decorative Visual   A graphic added for visual appeal. Decorative visuals do not promote the learning objective. See also Pumpkin Slide.

Drill and Practice   Assignment of repetitive practice exercises to help learners build automaticity.

Dual Channels   Feature of working memory referring to subcomponents devoted to visual information and to auditory information.

Effect Size   The difference in outcomes between a test group and a control group expressed as a multiplier of the standard deviation. Effect sizes of .3 and less are considered low; .3–.7 medium and .8 and above high.

Evidence-Based Practice   The conscientious, explicit, and judicious use of current best evidence in making decisions about learning environments that best support organizational goals.

Examples   An instance provided in a learning environment to illustrate a task or a content topic. Includes demonstrations. Also called worked examples.

Expertise Reversal   A condition in which an instructional method that helps novice learners either does not help or even hurts more experienced learners. For example, visuals improve learning of novices but not more experienced learners.

Explanations   Words in audio or text intended to teach content.

Explanatory Visuals   A visual that depicts relationships among the content elements. See also organizational, relational, transformational, and interpretive.

Facts   A type of knowledge that is unique and specific information about a person, place, or thing. The names of equipment parts or the features of a new product are two examples.

Faded Worked Examples   A series of examples that starts with a full worked example and gradually imposes more work on the learner ending with a full problem assignment.

Fading   See Faded Worked Exmples.

Feedback   Knowledge of results provided by the instruction typically in response to a practice exercise.

Graphics   A two- or three-dimensional visual representation of content. Includes static visuals such as line drawings and dynamic visuals such as animations.

Guided Discovery   See Immersive Architectures.

Immersive Architectures   Learning environments that are initiated by a realistic work task assignment and emphasize learning through experience. Also called whole task or experiential learning.

Implicit Instructional Methods   Training techniques that prompt mental processing leading to learning in the absence of behavioral activity. Relevant graphics are an example.

Interpersonal Skills   Tasks that involve interaction with others. Some examples include sales, teaching, customer service, and many management tasks. Also called social skills.

Intrinsic Feedback   Knowledge of results gleaned by seeing how a given action affects the environment. For example, after serving a tennis ball you can immediately see whether it landed where you intended. Often associated with immersive learning environments.

Instructional Architecture A design plan for a learning environment. Architectures vary regarding the amount and placement of learner interactions, the organization and size of lesson topics.

Instructional Media How learning environments are delivered to include instructors, computers, workbooks, and video.

Instructional Method A technique proven to make learning more effective or more efficient. Examples and practice are two important instructional methods addressed in this book.

Instructional Mode Three basic communication mechanisms: graphics, text, and audio.

Instructive Feedback Information provided by the learning environment regarding the correctness of the learner's response to a question or practice exercise.

Interpretive Graphic An explanatory visual that makes invisible phenomena visible. For example a graphic of molecules.

Learner-Centric View A focus on the strengths and limits of human memory in the design, development, and delivery of instructional programs. Contrast with Technology-centric View.

Learner Control The ability of the student to select the topics and manage the pacing of the learning environment. Asynchronous e-learning tends to be high in learner control where as instructor-led training tends to be low in learner control.

Learning Agent An onscreen image often placed in asynchronous e-learning courses.

Learning Host The recommended role of an instructor involving personable interactions with learners.

Learning Style Individual differences regarding how learners benefit from specific learning environments. Some of the more common learning styles include visual, auditory, and kinesthetic learners, the Myer's Briggs Inventory, and Kolb learning styles.

Level 1 Evaluation An assessment of the quality of a learning event based on participant opinions.

Long-term Memory Permanent memory. The repository of our knowledge and skills or mental models. Contains organized knowledge and skills in structures called schemas.

Massed Practice Organization of practice exercises in which most of the practice is assigned in one or two chunks. Contrast with spaced practice.

Media See Instructional Media.

Mental Load The amount of work imposed on working memory. When overloaded, working memory processing becomes inefficient. Also known as cognitive load.

Mental Model A representation of how something works stored in long-term memory. Mental models are the basis for understanding. Also known as schemas.

Meta-analysis A statistical technique in which multiple separate research studies are synthesized to allow more robust generalizations about specific instructional tactics.

Method See Instructional Methods

Mirror-Neuron System A part of the brain dedicated to learning movement skills by observation.

Mixed Practice An organization in which practice items that address several topics are assigned together.

Mode See Instructional Mode.

Organizational Graphic An explanatory visual that shows qualitative relationships among content topics. A tree diagram or a concept map are two examples.

Over-learning   Automaticity in task performance stemming from extensive practice.

Overt Activity   Visible actions taken by learners usually in response to a practice assignment.

Part-task Design   See Stair-Step Architectures.

Personalized Training   Learning environments that embed social cues such as first- and second-person language and human images.

Planning Phase   A stage in the creation of a presentation in which the sequence of topics, the introduction, and activities are specified. Usually takes the form of an outline.

Power Law of Practice   The relationship between the amount of practice and skill proficiency stating that proficiency continues to improve with continued practice but at diminishing rates.

Practice   Overt opportunities for learners to respond during a lesson in ways that support the objectives of the lesson. Diverse formats include multiple choice, drag and drop, projects, drill and practice, and so on.

Principled Presentation   An audio explanation by a speaker or narrator that incorporates proven instructional modes and methods to promote learning.

Problem-based Learning   A form of immersive learning architecture commonly used in medical education.

Procedures   Tasks that are performed more or less the same way each time they are done. Step-by-step routine tasks. Examples include logging onto your computer and following a recipe.

Process   A type of knowledge that depicts phases or stages of operation. How lightning forms and how equipment works are two examples.

Psychological Engagement   Mental processing in the service of learning.

Pumpkin Slides   Decorative visuals that do not promote the learning objective.

Recall Practice   Assignments that ask learners to repeat back content provided in the lesson. Also called regurgitation practice. Contrast with application practice.

Relational Graphic   An explanatory visual that summarizes quantitative data. Bar charts and pie graphs are common examples.

Retrieval   An essential phase of learning in which previously learned knowledge and skills are transferred from long-term memory into working memory when needed. Retrieval is the psychological basis for knowledge transfer.

Routine Tasks   See Procedures.

Scaffolding   Guidance included in lessons to reduce learner confusion and make learning more efficient. Scaffolding is especially needed in immersive learning architectures.

Scoping Phase   A stage in the creation of presentations in which the purpose of the presentation, features of the audience, and presentation setting are defined.

Show-and-Tell Architectures   Learning environments that rely primarily on explanations with few overt opportunities for learners to actively respond. Video documentaries and many lectures are typical examples.

Spaced Practice   Organization of practice assignments in which practice sessions are distributed throughout a lesson and among lessons.

Social Presence   The inclusion of interpersonal cues in a learning environment. Face to face environments typically have greatest potential for social presence while asynchronous e-learning has less.

Social Media   Computer applications that connect individuals in a personal way. Examples include Twitter and Facebook.

Stair-Step Architectures   Learning environments that divide content into small topics, provide practice and feedback after each topic, and generally provide high amounts of structure. Also called part-task learning. Most procedural training uses a stair-step approach.

Strategic Tasks   Tasks that are performed uniquely each time. These tasks require adaptation and problem solving to accommodate changes in the performance environment. Examples including making a sale and conducting a performance appraisal.

Supporting Topics   Concepts and factual knowledge needed to perform a task.

Synchronous e-learning   Computer-delivered instruction in which participants are geographically separate but online at the same time. Also called virtual classrooms. Contrast with asynchronous e-learning.

Technology-Centric View   A focus on the use of technology for learning often without regard for how technology features best support human learning processes.

Transfer   When new knowledge and skills acquired in a learning setting are retrieved and applied on the job, we say that transfer has occurred.

Transformational Graphic   An explanatory visual that shows changes in time or space. A cycle chart or animation of screen changes are two examples.

Varied Context Examples   A series of examples to illustrate a core principle in which the surface features of the examples change.

Visible Author Technique   Self-revelation by an instructor either in a face-to-face learning environment or in a text format.

Whole-Task Design   See Immersive Architectures.

Worked Examples   A step-by-step demonstration of how to solve a problem or complete a task.

Working Memory   Part of human memory that is responsible for conscious awareness, thinking, and learning. Working memory has a limited capacity and dual channels for visual and auditory information.

About the Author

Ruth Colvin Clark is determined to bridge the gap between academic research and practitioner application in instructional methods. A specialist in instructional design and workforce learning, she holds a doctorate in instructional psychology and served as training manager for Southern California Edison before founding her own company, Clark Training & Consulting. Clark was president of the International Society for Performance Improvement <http://www.ispi.org/> and received their Thomas Gilbert Distinguished Professional Achievement Award in 2006. She was selected as an ASTD Legend Speaker at the 2007 ICE Event. Her five other books also focus on various aspects of training and e-learning. Clark resides in Southwest Colorado and Phoenix, Arizona, and divides her time among speaking, teaching, and writing.

Index

technology, learning and the use of, 12–14, 242–243

text

bulleted, 104

placement, 104–106

versus audio explanations, 99–101

training, over inflated

checklist to avoid, 142

problem with, 128–130

training myths

evaluations of course/instructor and relationship to learning, 14–16, 243–244

instructional techniques, effectiveness of, 16–17, 244–245

learning styles, 10–12, 241–242

technology, use of, 12–14, 242–243

training surveys, 14–15

transfer of learning, 37–38, 65, 66–67

transformational visuals, 89, 90

U

U.S. Army, 13

V

varied context examples, 153

visible author technique, 118

visuals

See also explanations; graphics

applying, 91–92

explanatory, 89, 90

overuse of, 129–130

simple versus complex, 136–138

static versus animations, 138–140

voice quality, 121

W

Wetzell, K., 208

whole-task design. *See* immersive architectures

Woods, T., 162, 166

workforce learning, future for, 245–246

working memory

explanations and, 102–103

features of, 30–31

processing, 36, 65–66